Corporate Werewolf: A Survival Guide to Power, Office Politics, and Hidden Agendas

Verses Kindler Publication

Verses Kindler Publication.

Website: www.verseskindlerpublication.com

Corporate Werewolf: A Survival Guide to Power, Office Politics, and Hidden Agendas

By: Mr. James Donnelly

ISBN: 978-93-49532-09-0

1st Edition

Price: INR 349/$17.99

Disclaimer

Corporate Werewolf: A Survival Guide to Power, Office Politics, and Hidden Agendas is authored by James Donnelly. The entirety of this published work comprises the original content of the author, who has undertaken diligent efforts in its editing. The characters depicted herein may be fictitious or inspired by real events; however, they are not intended to cause offense or represent prejudice against any community or group. Any similarity to the names of actual individuals, locations, or institutions is purely coincidental and serves the narrative. The author bears sole responsibility for the originality of this work; the publisher assumes no liability thereof.

Index

Introduction to the Werewolf Game

How the social deduction game mirrors workplace politics

Not that your office is a workplace at all sometimes, it is a medieval village on trial, a vassal sweating, just before a torchlit trial, under a pale, suspicious moon. You could have believed that you were brought in to use your talents, when the truth is, you have simply been picked to play a game you were not aware was being conducted. And the game? It's Werewolf.

You know the setup. A group of people gathers together. By day, they chat and trade polite nods. By night, under the cover of darkness, some of them sprout claws and fangs. Werewolf is a social deduction game where players take on secret roles in a small village plagued by hidden werewolves. The game alternates between two phases—night and day—until one team wins.

Night Phase:

- All players close their eyes.
- Werewolves silently choose a player to eliminate.

Day Phase:

- All players open their eyes.
- The eliminated player is revealed and removed from the game.

Werewolves Win – When the number of werewolves equals or exceeds the number of villagers.

Villagers Win – When all werewolves have been eliminated.

No one knows who's who. The villagers try to protect their own, the werewolves work in secret to thin the herd, and every round is filled with accusations, alibis, and uneasy alliances. Someone gets "eliminated." The game resets. The tension never does.

Sound familiar?

It should. Swap the moonlit village for your open-plan office and the campfire whispers for WhatsApp or Slack threads, and you've got the same dynamic, just with fewer pitchforks and more performance reviews.

The Office as a Werewolf-Haunted Village

In both Werewolf and corporate life, the real game is not the work itself; it's the reading of the room and the masking of your own intent. The skill is not just doing the job, but surviving the pack.

You'll find:

- Werewolves in power suits, concealing their teeth behind PowerPoint slides.

- Villagers who trust too much and end up as pawns in a game they don't know they're playing.

- Spellcasters, werewolves who can turn a meeting into a hunt without ever raising their voice.

- Beta wolves, loyal followers, circling, waiting for a chance to move up in the pack.

Even the silences have meaning. In the wild, a wolf can stalk quietly for hours, waiting for the moment to strike. In the office, strategic silences in meetings can carry more weight than entire executive summaries...

The Politics of the Pack

Every organization has its villagers, the steady workers who keep the village running. They're the first in with coffee, the last to leave when a deadline looms. They believe that merit will protect them. They focus on delivering, not maneuvering.

But in the politics of the pack, villagers often end up the first to fall. Why?
Because Werewolves- like wolves in the wild- care less about the outcomes than they do about cementing their hierarchy. They miss the subtle power-tilting questions disguised as curiosity:

"I'm just wondering if your project is really aligned with the company's priorities?"

"Do we have the right person leading this?"

A wolf doesn't attack the strongest prey first; it takes the unguarded, the ones not looking over their shoulder. In the workplace, the villagers are those who don't watch the shadows. And in wolf logic, unguarded means expendable.

The Werewolves: Charming, Calculated, and Pack-Minded

Werewolves, like their wild cousins, are bound to the same instincts that govern wolf packs—hierarchy, alliance, and the constant struggle for dominance. Werewolves in the workplace are predators in plain sight. They can compliment your work in one breath and plant seeds of doubt about your "fit" in the next. They don't lunge. They circle. They use plausible deniability like fur in the winter, warm, protective, and impossible to peel away without a fight.

They don't lie outright. They tilt the truth, just enough to warp perception:

"I've heard some concerns..."

"People are wondering if..."

"I just want to flag something early..."

In the wild, a wolf masks its scent by camouflaging itself with the scent of its surroundings, and so also does a Corporate Werewolf mask its presence through the social camouflage of alliances, flattery, and false humility. They move in ways that hide intent. You never see the attack coming until your reputation is bleeding in the snow.

And they never hunt alone. Wolves work in coordinated silence. One distracts while the other positions. One builds trust while another undermines. By the time you realize you're surrounded, the case for your demise has already been built.

Why It's the Same Game

The core of both Werewolf and workplace politics is not just hidden identity, but hidden intention and shifting trust. In the game, you survive by knowing when to speak, when to accuse, and when to feign innocence. In business, it's the same, except no one ever hands you a card that says:

"You're the outsider today. Try not to look suspicious while doing your job."

Instead, you walk into Monday's stand-up scanning faces like a hunter assessing threats in the dark woods:

Who's genuinely on my side?

Who's just waiting for me to slip?

Who's smiling because they mean it, and who's smiling because they smell blood, their senses sharpened by the scent of vulnerability?

And then you see that coworker, the one who always volunteers first, always has a polished answer, always seems to "just know" what leadership wants. Are they simply enthusiastic? Or are they the corporate equivalent of a wolf in sheep's clothing?

From Coffee Breaks to Moonlit Hunts

It's not just the big moves that matter; it's the small ones.

A "random" reshuffle that quietly shifts influence.

A casual question in a meeting that changes the narrative.

A private Slack DM that suddenly makes you second-guess your standing.

A werewolf may leave some slight traces in the village, a track in the snow, a rustling in the bushes. Those manifestations in the office are half-sentences and hesitations. The majority pays no attention to them, yet they are considered benign. That is the way that the werewolves prosper.

Congratulations, You're a Player

The moment you recognize these patterns, you stop being "just an employee" and start being a player in the real game. Every meeting becomes a round. Every silence could be a strategy. Every smile could be genuine, or it could be masking teeth.

The question isn't whether the game is happening. It's whether you're awake enough to see it.

The Seers: Eyes That See Through the Trees

In every wolf-haunted village, there are a rare few who can see beyond the flicker of the firelight. They don't just hear the obvious howl in the distance; they can tell which direction it came from, how many wolves there are, and how close they are to making their move.

These are the Seers.

In the corporate game, Seers are the people who read the room before the room even knows what it's feeling. They catch the twitch of an eyebrow when a proposal lands poorly. They notice the "out of office" block that conveniently appears right before an announcement about restructuring. They can smell the shift in the wind before the first leaf falls.

But here's the curse of the Seer: knowledge is dangerous. In the Werewolf game, revealing too much too soon gets you targeted by the wolves. In the office, it's the same. Call out the truth too boldly, and you mark yourself as a threat. Keep silent too long, and you fade into irrelevance.

As in the game Werewolf, Seers walk a knife's edge, or in wolf terms, a narrow ridge in the snow. One wrong step to the left, and the pack drags you down. One wrong step to the right, and you fall into the cold, unseen. The art is offering just enough insight to remain valuable, but never so much that others feel exposed or endangered by your vision.

The Alliance Shuffle: Wolves Change Sides Quickly

In Werewolf, alliances form quickly because survival demands it. "You can trust me," someone says with steady eyes and an open palm. And maybe you can, for one night. But in the world of wolves, loyalty is not a virtue; it's a convenience.

Corporate alliances are no different. Today's ally might be your fiercest defender in a meeting, circling with you to fend off a rival wolf. But the moment incentives shift, when a promotion appears, when leadership favors someone else, when the scent of opportunity carries on the wind, that same ally may pivot and bare their teeth at you.

This is not betrayal in the wolf's mind. It is survival. It is the instinct to follow the strongest scent of advantage.

In the real world, temporary alliances often masquerade as friendship. You share projects, goals, and late-night war stories over drinks. But make no mistake, this is chess, not checkers. Sharing the same square today does not mean you won't be their next move tomorrow. In wolf packs, dominance is tested constantly, and the same happens in the office. The pack dynamic is fluid, and yesterday's running mate can be tomorrow's rival without a single howl of warning.

The Silent Strategy: When the Wolf Doesn't Howl

Loud wolves draw hunters, alerting them to their presence. Emotional wolves expose their position. But the quiet ones? They endure initial scrutiny.

In both Werewolf and corporate life, selective silence is not the absence of strategy; it is the sharpening of it. A wolf in the wild may lie low in the dark timber for hours, watching, listening, waiting for the perfect moment to strike. In the office, the quiet player uses silence to let others reveal themselves first. They take in the tension, watch who leans toward whom, and see where the power lines run.

But timing matters. Stay too quiet for too long, and you risk becoming invisible, and in this game, invisibility can mean vulnerability. A wolf that never hunts eventually starves.

Silence creates space, and in that space, the smart players gather information and prepare for the inevitable storm. When the political wind shifts, and it always shifts, these quiet wolves are ready to pivot without looking desperate or lost.

The Hidden Pack Rules

Here's the truth: if you can't learn the hidden rules, you're not sitting out the game, you're simply being played.

Corporate life hands you an official playbook: mission statements, quarterly targets, leadership principles. That's the script they want you to believe runs the village. But beneath it lies the real werewolf code, the unspoken hierarchies, the legacy loyalties, and the silent rivalries that dictate who rises and who gets pushed out to the frozen edge.

When you understand this hidden code, you can:

- Smell the danger before it reaches you.
- Predict the moves of those who circle closest.
- Avoid becoming a scapegoat for the pack's mistakes.
- Hunt for promotions, pivots, and influence without stumbling into the traps of fear-based control.

And no, awareness doesn't make you manipulative; it makes you prepared. Wolves endure by understanding the rhythms of the hunt; fail to read it, and you're not avoiding the pack—you're feeding it!

The Endless Daylight of Corporate Werewolf

In the game of Werewolf, night is when the real moves are made. But in corporate life, there is no night. The game plays on under endless daylight, and the players never take off their masks. There are no convenient "reveal" rounds where everyone shows their cards.

That gut feeling you've been ignoring? It's the same instinct that keeps a lone wolf alive on the tundra. It's telling you who to trust, who to avoid, and when to step back from the fire before the hunt turns your way.

Knowing the game doesn't make you sneaky; it makes you a SEER.

And in this world, the choice isn't whether to play or not. The moment you joined the pack, the decision was made for you. The only question left is: will you play with your eyes closed... or will you learn to see in the dark?

Chapter 1 - Welcome to the Village!

In the village, shadows creep,

Whispers stir while others sleep.

Deceit takes root in darkened air,

A Werewolf prowls, but who's aware?

By dawn's first light, the doubts arise,

Truth entangled, masked in lies.

The Seer warns, the crowd resists,

Yet fate is sealed within their midst.

A vote is cast, a name is called,

The wrong is right, the brave enthralled.

One by one, the trusted fall,

Fear and silence claim them all.

Yet listen close, heed well the game,

Not all who lead play fair the same.

A silver tongue, a cunning mind,

Can twist the truth, and leave trust behind.

So, watch, dear friend, and learn with care,

For wolves in suits of virtue wear.

And should you find yourself in doubt,

Speak up soon, or be cast out!

Werewolf as a Metaphor for Corporate Life

At first glance, the modern workplace looks like a well-fed, well-groomed pack. Everyone wears their professional coats, pressed shirts, neat hair, and LinkedIn-ready smiles. The policies are polished, the org chart lines run straight, and every title has an air of authority. It's all very grown-up, very civilized.

But step beyond the welcome email, past the glossy quarterly town hall, and you'll realize you're not in a peaceful pasture. You've wandered into a clearing in the dark forest, surrounded by watchful eyes. The corporate world is not just a job; it's a living, breathing game of Werewolf, where trust is the most valuable currency, silence can be a weapon, and not everything is as it seems.

In Werewolf, no one's role is obvious. Some players hide sharp teeth behind warm smiles. Others pretend to be powerless while pulling the pack's strings. The real game unfolds not in the open meeting but in the whispers between calls, the subtle glance across the table, the "we should catch up" coffee invites that carry more than caffeine.

Sound familiar? That's because in most offices, survival isn't just about hitting your KPIs, it's about reading the pack. It's spotting the alpha who doesn't have a title, the beta waiting to challenge them, and the lone wolf who looks harmless until the lights go out. The best survivors are not the loudest barkers or the most skilled hunters; they're the ones who know when to growl, when to blend into the trees, and when to quietly fall in step with the wolf who really leads the hunt.

PowerPoint decks and Excel sheets are the visible tracks in the snow. Beneath them lies the real terrain, WhatsApp DMs, hallway pacts, whispered strategy sessions over lattes. This isn't chaos. It's the natural order of the corporate wild.

So how do you survive *Corporate Werewolf*? You don't have to howl the loudest or bare your fangs at every turn. You need to become a tracker. Read the unspoken trails. Learn which wolves trust each other, which circles are safe to enter, and which fires you should never approach. Use your influence like a hunter uses the wind, carefully, invisibly. Guard your reputation as a wolf guards its den.

Here's the twist: those who master this aren't just better hunters, they're better leaders. They use their position not to manipulate, but to create a stronger pack. They understand that the real win isn't just surviving the hunt, it's reshaping the hunt so fewer wolves need to turn on each other to eat.

The Psychological Forces at Play: Why the Pack Behaves the Way It Does

Why does your office sometimes feel like a game of social deduction around a campfire?

Picture it: it's Pizza Friday, but the mood feels like the moon just shifted. You're in the break area, balancing a limp slice, trying to sniff out the change in the air. Someone casually mentions "budget cuts" and "travel bans." Another wolf suddenly finds their soda can *very* interesting. The one who usually howls the loudest about company gossip? Dead silent. This isn't lunch. This is a hunt.

Is Cristina praising your latest project because she respects you, or because she's marking you as prey for the next performance review? Is Tom forgetting your name for the third time an innocent slip, or a way to make you feel smaller in the pecking order?

In Werewolf, the tension lies in suspicion, shifting alliances, and the split-second judgments that can save or sink you. The corporate world runs on the same primal currents, only the howls are replaced by calendar invites and "quick chats."

Groupthink: The Power (and Danger) of the Pack

In the Werewolf circle, the danger begins when suspicion turns to certainty, and certainty turns into a mob. One wolf points a paw at you, and suddenly, the pack is growling for your elimination. You know you're innocent, but every word in your defense just makes your fur stand out more. So you lower your head, nod along with the alpha's judgment, and hope they turn their teeth elsewhere next round.

That's groupthink, the instinct to move with the pack, even when the trail feels wrong. In the office, it's the meeting where the alpha declares a shaky idea "brilliant," and the rest of the wolves nod rather than risk being the one who challenges the leader's scent trail. It's safety in numbers, but also danger in numbers, because the pack can charge straight into a cliff if no one dares to howl a warning.

Real-World Cautionary Tale – The Challenger Disaster

In 1986, NASA was on the verge of history. But behind the scenes, engineers had smelled danger; the O-rings might fail in cold weather. They raised concerns. The Werewolves in leadership, under pressure from political predators and public expectations, dismissed them. The pack followed. The shuttle launched. Seventy-three seconds later, the sky split apart.

The tragedy wasn't just a mechanical failure; it was a failure of the pack to listen to its cautious scouts. Groupthink silenced the lone howls that might have saved the hunt.

Lesson for the workplace: when your gut says the trail is wrong, risk the growl. Better to be the wolf who howled too soon than the one who watched the pack run into the trap.

Confirmation Bias: Hunting What You Expect to Find

In Werewolf, once a player decides you're suspicious, every twitch of your ear becomes "evidence." You shift in your chair? Wolf move. You speak too quickly? Wolf move. Even the truth sounds like deception when the pack has already decided you're the threat and must be diminished.

That's confirmation bias, our brain's tendency to hunt for tracks that fit the prey we've already decided to chase.

Corporate Example – BlackBerry's Blind Trail

Once, Blackberry was the undisputed alpha of the smartphone territory. When the Apple pack strode silently into the clearing with a touchscreen, BlackBerry's leaders laughed. "Our Wolves love buttons," they insisted. "Touchscreens are just a passing scent in a high wind." They ignored every sign of shifting prey patterns, hunting only along the trails they already knew.

The touchscreen wasn't a fad. It was a kill shot. And Blackberry, blinded by its own bias, became carrion for the next generation of mobile device hunters.

In the workplace, confirmation bias can make you miss the true threats or dismiss the real opportunities, because you're too busy sniffing the wrong scent.

The Blackberry Blind Spot: Howling at the Wrong Moon

Despite the scent of change thick in the air, iPhone sales surging, the app ecosystem exploding, users practically howling for bigger screens and sleeker designs, Blackberry kept sniffing around the same old hunting grounds. They doubled down on their pack's old hunting method: the physical keyboard. Their belief? "Real predators use claws, not touchscreens."

Reality? The herd had moved. Consumers wanted vast hunting ranges (more screen), fewer barriers (no buttons), and the addictive chase of Angry Birds.

By the time Blackberry realized the prey had migrated, they were left panting behind, chasing ghosts, like the Werewolf player still insisting Steve's guilty long after he's been tossed from the village.

The lesson: When your instincts become stubborn like an alpha refusing to change territory, it's time to pause, lift your head to the wind, and scent the full truth of the landscape. If you only follow the trail you *want* to see, you'll go hungry.

Fear and Mistrust: Living in a Perpetual Full Moon

In the Werewolf game, paranoia spreads like wildfire in dry brush. The moon rises, and suddenly, your closest packmate is baring their teeth. Every sideways glance feels like a challenge. You spend half the night circling each other, the other half regretting the wrong bite.

Now picture that same tension at your 9-to-5.

In certain corporate forests, the full moon never sets. Leadership stays cryptic, decisions are made deep in the shadows, and information trickles out like scraps from a kill. Before long, the den is restless. Colleagues turn into lone wolves, hoarding knowledge like meat in winter. Gossip runs through the ranks like a pack on the hunt, but instead of chasing opportunity, they're chasing answers.

Example – The Toxic Pack

In fear-led companies, wolves pad softly, always on guard. Strategy meetings feel like alpha challenges, and innovation dies in the cold because no one wants to risk being the one who spoke up and got isolated. The best hunters? They slip away to another pack before the howling gets worse.

Moral: A pack united in trust hunts well. A pack divided by fear just circles each other until the prey escapes.

Persuasion and Influence: Controlling the Hunt

In Werewolf, the best predator isn't always the one with the sharpest teeth; it's the one who controls the howl. The werewolf who convinces the others that the scent trail leads elsewhere survives another night.

In the corporate world, narrative control works the same way. A charismatic alpha wolf can rally the pack, set the direction, and get everyone chasing the same prey. But persuasion cuts both ways. The same charm that unites can also mislead.

The Steve Jobs Effect

Jobs was a master alpha; in werewolf parlance, he was part Spellcaster, part Illusionist, and he could make the pack believe they could leap canyons. His "reality distortion field" didn't just sell devices; it rewired belief. Hunters ran faster, leapt higher, chased prey they didn't know existed. But here's the danger: when the alpha starts believing their own myth too much, they can lead the pack straight into a trap.

Takeaway: Influence is a powerful howl. Use it to lead the hunt, not to mask the dangers on the trail.

Case Study: Enron – A Wolf's Den Built on Illusion

Imagine a glittering wolf den on the edge of the forest. From the outside, it's thriving, sleek fur, plentiful kills, powerful alphas. But inside? Bones are brittle, the prey count is falsified, and the scent of rot is everywhere.

Jeffrey Skilling and Ken Lay weren't just leaders; they were illusionists, masking a famine with the smell of feasts. The pack smelled something off. The blood was too sweet, the kills too easy. But groupthink, that dangerous lull where the pack follows without question, kept everyone quiet.

The few wolves who growled in warning? Silenced or exiled. Loyalty was rewarded; truth was punished. And so the pack hunted blindly... until the cliff's edge came. When Enron fell, it wasn't just the alphas who perished; the entire pack scattered, and the forest remembered.

Lesson: When the meat smells wrong, don't keep chewing. Trust your nose, even if the alpha says otherwise.

Secrets to Becoming a Lunar Leader

Most workplaces shouldn't feel like a blood moon hunt where every shadow hides a rival. But too many packs live that way. That's where the Lunar Leader rises.

The Lunar Leader understands the wild. They know the scent of fear, the posture of deception, the rustle of danger in the undergrowth. But instead of biting first, they pause. They listen. They move the pack with quiet authority, not domination.

The full moon doesn't just stir chaos; it casts long shadows where truth stands revealed. A Lunar Leader uses that light to see through the noise, to call the pack to higher ground, to guide them where prey is plentiful and the dangers are known.

They're not fooled by the silver-tongued werewolf or the shifting alliances in the underbrush. They lead with clarity, courage, and the instinct to protect as much as to pursue.

Key Parallels Between Werewolf and Business (Wolf Edition)

1. **Trust & Deception**

   A pack without trust is just a cluster of lone wolves. The wrong alpha can turn the hunt into a pack in chaos.

2. **Decision-Making in the Fog**

The forest is thick. You can't see every threat, but you must choose your path.

3. **Roles & Hidden Power**

The biggest wolf isn't always the leader; sometimes the smallest holds the sharpest mind.

4. **Communication & Miscommunication**

A poorly timed howl can send the prey running.

5. **Adaptability = Survival**

Seasons change. Prey moves. The pack that can pivot survives.

Final Howl: The Game Within the Pack

Werewolf isn't just a game of social deduction. It's a crash course in reading the wind, sensing danger, rallying allies, and leading through uncertainty. Business, stripped to the bone, is no different. It's human behavior with a thin veneer of pin stripes.

Next time your team gathers, maybe don't just run a trust exercise, run a game of werewolf, and make sure your leaders play. Watch who speaks, who waits, who follows the wrong scent, and who keeps the pack together when the moon rises.

In every workplace, there are a few werewolves. The real question is: will you become a Lunar Leader (the alpha who leads), the lone wolf who simply survives, or the prey that gets hunted?

Chapter 2 - Centers of Authority

They circle close with polished grace,

Each smile rehearsed, each glance a brace.

They kneel not out of earned respect,

But to survive, to self-protect.

Loyalties sold, and fear is spent,

Obedience forged through false consent.

Not truth, but silence oils the gears,

A whisper-fed machine of fears.

And shadows reign where lights delayed,

In courts where trust is long betrayed.

Why Do People Cluster Around Toxic Leaders? (Spoiler: It's Not About the Free Donuts)

In the asymmetrical landscape of corporate life, some leaders inspire, some mentor, and then, there are those who rule with the subtlety of a flamethrower. These are toxic leaders. Think less Captain America, more Cersei Lannister. You know, the ones who confuse fear with respect and treat feedback like a personal attack.

And yet, people still gather around them. They defend them. Promote their ideas. Even mimic their behavior. But why?

Let's dissect the psychology, the strategy, and the unfortunate survival instincts behind this phenomenon.

"If I'm close to them, I'm safe," they think.

Or at least, "If I'm close, I'll see the fireball coming first."

The Gravitational Pull of Power (Even If It's Radioactive)

Toxic leaders aren't liked, but they are feared, and that's half the job done. In high-pressure environments, staying close to power often feels like a winning strategy. It's like cosying up to a dragon, not because you love fire, but because you'd rather not be on the receiving end of it.

They command attention the way villains do in a good thriller; you don't root for them, but you can't look away. And in organizations where status, promotions, and paychecks are on the line, proximity often trumps principles.

Survival Over Sincerity: Enter the Corporate Muzzle

Toxic leaders thrive in environments where people stop speaking the truth and start echoing what they think the leader wants to hear. It's not alignment, it's fear wearing a business suit.

They send subtle (or not-so-subtle) messages:

"Speak up, and you're out."

"Disagree, and watch your responsibilities disappear."

"Be loyal, and you might make it."

Employees don't comply because they believe, they comply because it's safer than becoming the office example of "what happens when you cross the boss." I call this the corporate muzzle: an invisible gag that gets tighter the closer you get to the corner office.

Amazon's Corporate Werewolf Game: When Performance Feels Like Paranoia

Scene One: Welcome to Camp Amazon

Imagine showing up to work where everyone smiles, but you can't subdue the feeling that they're watching your every move.

Your ideas are questioned, your tone is dissected, and Slack messages are mined like FBI transcripts.

Behold the grand illusion that is Amazon: a corporate game of Werewolf, cleverly cosplaying as your dream job.

In this high-stakes version of the party game, coworkers aren't just colleagues, they're competitors, and everyone's playing to survive the next performance review.

The Game Setup: Amazon's Work Culture

In 2015, the New York Times revealed what insiders already knew: working at Amazon could feel like a twisted reality show where:

- Critique is currency
- Kindness is risky
- And loyalty is temporary

Amazon had built a fortress of efficiency. But the bricks? Long hours, internal competition, and a culture of relentless feedback, often harsh and public.

And let's not forget the twist: you could be voted out of the Village (aka, performance-managed out) at any time.

Strategy Guide: The Werewolf Rules of Amazon

In the party game Werewolf, players must:

- Find and eliminate the impostors
- Argue, accuse, and defend themselves
- And do all of this while pretending to work together

At Amazon, the same rules applied.

Employees were incentivized to challenge one another, sometimes unethically, in meetings. If your teammate had a flawed idea? You'd be rewarded for tearing it apart. Not personally, of course, just professionally enough to count as feedback.

Just like in Werewolf, Trust no one became the unspoken motto. Alliances were shaky, friendships fragile, and everyone's eyes were on the prize: not being the next one "voted off the island."

The MET Index: Where's the Teamwork?

The MET Index (Management, Empowerment, Teamwork) reveals how Amazon stacked up:

- *Management*: Fierce, direct, and results-driven. Bezos set the tone with his now-infamous phrase: "Are you lazy or just incompetent?"

- *Empowerment*: Sure, Amazon gave you ownership. But it also gave you stress-induced Sunday night dread and the joy of checking emails during family dinners and time off.

- *Teamwork*: The kind of teamwork that resembles a Hunger Games alliance, friendly until you're both up for the same promotion.

Winning the Game: At What Cost?

This ultra-competitive setup worked... sort of.

- Amazon grew fast. Really fast.
- It topped performance charts and climbed the Fortune 500.
- It innovated, disrupted, and dominated.

But...

People burned out.

Women didn't rise through the ranks because who has time to raise a family when your phone pings 24/7?

Older employees feared replacement by younger, commitment-free werewolves-in-training.

And ex-Amazonians? Sometimes seen as too intense, too critical, too... well, Amazonian.

Public Scrutiny: When the Village Woke Up

The NYT article hit like a spotlight in a dark forest. Suddenly, the villagers (I.e., the public) were pointing fingers, not at any individual, but at the game itself.

Jeff Bezos, the game master, had to defend Amazon's culture. But the damage was done. The brand took a hit, and potential recruits started wondering, "Is the paycheck worth the paranoia?"

Can You Win Without Turning Into a Werewolf?

The brilliance of Amazon's model lies in its results, but excellence doesn't always translate to balance. When the workplace starts to feel like a psychological thriller, where each meeting carries the tension of an elimination round, then success is no longer about thriving, but simply surviving.

In a world that increasingly values collaboration, emotional intelligence, and psychological safety, Amazon's Werewolf-style culture raises a hard question: What kind of performance are we really rewarding?

When paranoia becomes part of the job description, companies risk creating high-output machines powered by burnt-out humans. And the biggest irony? In trying to weed out the "weak," they often lose the wise, the empathetic, and the quietly brilliant.

Because in the end, if you have to constantly look over your shoulder, you're not leading the future, you're just outlasting it.

If Amazon wants to keep growing without chewing through its talent pool, it might need to change the game.

Maybe replace Werewolf with something else.

Something a little more... human.

Manufactured Urgency = Manipulation Masterclass

Toxic leaders are rarely chill. They thrive on chaos and false deadlines. Everything is urgent, critical, or mission-defining. This keeps the team reactive instead of reflective. And when you're running around putting out fires all day, you don't have time to ask: "Wait... why are we even on fire?"

By keeping everyone in panic mode, they ensure loyalty through dependency. It's leadership through exhaustion. Just like players in Werewolf start accusing others to avoid suspicion, employees under toxic leaders throw each other under the bus, hoping to buy themselves more time in the leader's favor.

Why This Cycle Repeats

Toxic leaders rarely build sustainable teams; they structure echo chambers. Their style pushes out those with integrity and promotes those who toe the line. Over time, the culture reshapes itself around the dysfunction:

HR stops challenging behavior, especially of leaders.

Teams stop innovating and start appeasing.

New hires either adapt or self-select out.

And unless someone high up hits the big red "Cultural Reset" button, this cycle keeps spinning. Like a bad sequel nobody asked for.

The Psychology Behind It All

Let's break down a few psychological levers toxic leaders use like a maestro with a dark orchestra:

1. *Fear of exclusion*: Humans are social beings. Being outcast from the group, especially professionally, feels like emotional death.

2. *Reward-based conditioning*: "You were loyal? Here's a title bump." Pavlov would be proud.

3. *Moral disengagement*: "The game's evolved." "Maybe it's you who's stuck in yesterday." and "We need people who are more digitally fluent." Slowly, ethics erode under pressure.

So, What Can Be Done?

If you're in this orbit, the solution isn't just to "be brave" because bravery without backup gets you burned. Instead:

1. Build alliances with others who value integrity. There's safety in numbers.

2. Document everything, cover your tail, or find it's been chewed off!

3. Raise concerns strategically, ideally with support or when leverage is on your side.

4. Look for exits if the culture is deeply entrenched. You're not a tree. You can move.

Remember - Loyalty Isn't Leadership

Following a toxic leader doesn't make you strategic; it makes you stuck. The real power lies in seeing the game for what it is, refusing to play dirty, and helping create spaces where leadership is about trust, not tactics.

Because the only thing worse than a toxic leader... is becoming one.

Loyalty Points: Redeem for Promotions, Praise & Peril

Step inside the world of Toxic Leadership Inc., where loyalty isn't just valued, it's the secret handshake to success. Forget talent, innovation, or results. If you want to climb the corporate ladder here, there's only one requirement: pledge allegiance to the boss's ego.

Toxic leaders don't just rule by fear; they sweeten the deal. Promotions, public praise, and "accidentally" overhearing top-secret strategies become the rewards for those who toe the line. It's like a twisted version of Willy Wonka's chocolate factory, where golden tickets are handed out, but only to those who nod the hardest and question the least.

Think of it this way: in real estate, it's "location, location, location." In toxic workplaces? It's "loyalty, loyalty, loyalty."

True loyalty isn't blind; it's built on shared purpose, mutual respect, and courage under pressure. In high-trust teams led by Lunar Leaders, loyalty becomes a strategic advantage. It's rooted in customer obsession, a bold vision, and mutual accountability. It flourishes when leaders stand between their teams and the chaos, between the werewolves and the village, shielding their people from politics and predators.

Here, loyalty is directed toward the mission, the customers, and the team's higher purpose, not toward protecting egos. Success is measured by impact and integrity, not by political games.

The difference? Toxic loyalty protects power. True loyalty propels purpose.

Example: The Cult of Loyalty in High-Pressure Work Zones

In some fast-paced offices, it's less "collaboration" and more "courtroom drama", with everyone auditioning to be the leader's most devoted disciple. Promotions go to the yes-men. Praise is reserved for the sycophants. And if you dare to ask, "Is this the best approach?" Well, you'd better start packing your desk plant.

Just look at the headlines. Scandals in finance, tech, and healthcare often have a common thread: insiders who spotted red flags but zipped their lips. Why? Because questioning the boss risks everything. But turning a blind eye? That earns you a seat at the table... until the house of cards collapses.

The irony? True high risers aren't in the business of putting speed bumps in the way of leadership; they're in the business of putting passing lanes in to accelerate the boss's plans. They don't blindly agree; they think critically, offer better routes, and help leaders reach their goals faster and stronger.

Werewolf at Work

It's like a game of Werewolf. You know someone's being shady, but siding with the alpha gives you temporary protection. So you play along, align with the loudest voice, and hope they don't turn on you. But spoiler alert: in both Werewolf and toxic workplaces, when the tide turns, loyalty won't save you. You're still a target, just a slower-moving one.

Always remember, in workplaces where praise and promotions are tied to loyalty, not merit, you're not building a career, you're playing a dangerous game of survival. And eventually, even the most loyal players get voted off the island when performance fails to meet expectations.

The Illusion of Safety: Snuggling Up to Power Won't Keep You Warm Forever

You've seen it. Maybe you've lived it. The classic survival move in a toxic environment: cozying up to the leader, thinking proximity equals protection. "If I'm close enough to the throne," you tell yourself, "I can dodge the daggers."

But here's the twist: in toxic kingdoms, even the jester gets beheaded.

We call it The Illusion of Safety, the seductive belief that being the trusted confidant, the right-hand advisor, the whisperer behind the curtain, will somehow let you steer the storm. But in reality? You're just sitting closer to the eye of the hurricane.

Enter Machiavelli: The OG Prince of Werewolves

In The Prince, Niccolò Machiavelli penned what many see as the ultimate manual for ruthless power plays. His take? It's better to be feared than loved. Why? Because fear, he claimed, is predictable. Controllable.

This idea has seeped into boardrooms, politics, and break rooms with surprisingly little resistance. Toxic leaders absorb it like gospel, crafting cultures where fear keeps people quiet, pliable, obedient. And yet... This system is like playing with fireworks in a dry forest, dramatic, sure, but wildly unstable.

The Werewolf Paradox

Think of it like the game Werewolf. You ally with the beast early on, thinking, "We're in this together!" You help them eliminate threats, cheer on their deceit, and feel clever in your calculated loyalty.

But then... surprise! You're next.

Why? Because the moment your usefulness fades, or your influence grows just a tad too strong, the werewolf doesn't hesitate. Loyalty means nothing to a creature that thrives on control. You were a pawn, not a partner.

Real Power Is Knowing When to Step Back

True safety doesn't lie in clutching the coattails of power; it lies in discernment. In knowing when to stand near power and when to stand apart from it. Appeasement might buy you time, but never security.

So next time you're tempted to play the game of toxic allegiance, remember: the closer you dance to the flame, the more likely you are to burn.

Breaking the Cycle: The Antidote to Fear-Based Leadership

Let's get real, fear-based leadership is like using duct tape to fix a sinking ship. Sure, it might hold for a while, but sooner or later, things start leaking... and then? Splash. Total collapse.

But here's the good news: there is an antidote. It's not found in boardroom power plays or whispered threats; it's in something I like to call Lunar Leadership. Why lunar? Because it reflects light in darkness, it influences tides (read: people), and it doesn't need to scream to be noticed.

Let's break it down:

1. Recognizing Manipulative Tactics

Every good revolution starts with awareness. Toxic leaders are masters of psychological chess: they move pawns through fear-mongering, create fake urgency like a fire drill for a candle, sideline top performers like it's a Hunger Games spin-off, and reward loyalty over logic.

Training employees to spot these patterns isn't optional; it's self-defense.

2. Building a Culture of Accountability

Forget top-down dictates from the "Ivory Tower of Doom." Healthy organizations hold leaders accountable through a shared culture of radical transparency. This isn't about pitchforks and drama; it's about creating systems where feedback flows freely, and leadership decisions are weighed on the scale of ethics, not ego.

3. Empowering Ethical Leadership

Want innovation, resilience, and actual progress? You won't get it with intimidation. Organizations that invest in developing leaders rooted in trust and collaboration are the ones that thrive, even when budgets are tight and the coffee machine is broken again.

(Trust me: esprit de corps can outperform espresso.)

Here's the truth: fear-based leadership is a ticking time bomb in a velvet box. It might sparkle on the outside, but eventually, it will result in a "boom". Like the Werewolf party game, deception gets exposed, alliances shift, and the crowd turns. The question isn't if the toxic leader will fall... It's when.

So, do you want to be part of the house of mirrors or help build the lighthouse?

Remember, empowerment isn't just about giving authority or resources; its true essence lies in recognizing and rewarding those who lead with integrity, fairness, and a genuine sense of responsibility. It's a commitment to shining a light on ethical leadership and inspiring others to follow their example.

Final Thought

If your job feels like a strategic trust fall... with no one behind you, maybe it's not "team-building", possibly, it's a trap. And if the only people getting ahead are those fluent in flattery and fear, then it might be time to brush up on your resume instead of your loyalty points.

Just remember: in the wild world of toxic workplaces, playing the game might keep you in it, but refusing to play might just help you win.

Coming up next:

We'll venture into the mysterious world of workplace "shadow councils", those unofficial influencers who pull strings behind the scenes. We'll talk about how real leaders can expose (or empower) these hidden networks to either uphold or heal the soul of an organization.

Keep reading, stay tuned. The moonlight's just getting started...

Chapter 3 - The Shadow Council Paradox: Ally or Saboteur?

"Beware the ones who lurk behind,

With power masked, yet well-defined.

For those who rule yet wear no crown,

May lift you up or pull you down."

The Influence of Unseen Leadership

Every office has that person. No fancy title, no corner office, no direct reports, but decisions don't move without their discreet nod. Promotions manifest after a coffee chat. Conflicts dissolve before reaching escalation. They shape outcomes like a playwright rewriting scenes mid-show.

Hey, come on in! This is the invisible boardroom. The world of the Shadow Council welcomes you!

Power Without Position

Not all leaders sit atop the organizational chart. Some wield influence with sleight-of-hand precision, working in the background to steer the ship. They are executive assistants who know everything, product managers whose "suggestions" quietly become directives, veteran engineers no one dares cross, and HR managers who subtly recalibrate team dynamics.

They don't command; they suggest. They don't instruct; they influence. Their currency is trust, timing, and perception.

The Werewolf Analogy: Hidden Roles, Real Power

In the game of Werewolf, most play at face value, unaware of those with hidden roles and knowledge, manipulating the game. The Shadow Council operates similarly with off-the-record conversations, subtle alliances, and carefully placed words. To outsiders, it seems like a coincidence. But to insiders, it's choreography.

A raised eyebrow. A strategic "For Your Information (FYI)." Silence at the right moment.

These are the tools of influence.

Archetypes of the Shadow Council

Every informal network has its roles:

- The Whisperer - Master of hallway diplomacy. Never loud, always heard.

- The Architect – The Invisible Engineer of Alignment. They don't chase influence, the rational builder of frameworks.

- The Sheep Dog - Shields fragile teams or leaders, often stabilizing chaos.

- The Puppeteer - Orchestrates from the sidelines. Others speak; they echo the Puppeteer.

- The Joker - The wildcard. Lighthearted on the surface, but tracking everything. Their jokes carry intel (subtle truths, criticisms, or insights).

These individuals aren't anomalies; they are often the pulse of the culture.

The Invisible Hand: Meet Your Organization's Secret Operating System

Forget the organizational chart. Ignore the mission statements. And definitely leave behind that awkward town hall where leadership unveiled a 53-slide strategy deck.

While the spotlight shines on official titles and glossy PowerPoints, real influence is brewing quietly in the breakroom, the group chat, and those oh-so-casual walks to the coffee machine.

It's the Shadow Council, the organization's backstage navigators, who don't just react to power. They reroute it.

They're your team leads, domain experts, product whisperers, and quietly trusted lieutenants. They've got enough title to be in the room and enough experience to actually matter once they're there.

They don't always have C-suite access, but they've got something better: a proven track record of success, which gives them access to the ear of C-suite members and the trust of the floor (village). They're fluent in both languages - vision-speak and day-to-day reality, and they specialize in translation. Upstream, they shape the story. Downstream, they influence the execution.

These folks don't schedule meetings; conversations just happen. No one takes minutes, but actions mysteriously shift. No one announces a decision, but everyone starts following it.

They're the unofficial think tank, the silent influencers, the walking "corporate rutter" that subtly tilts policy, direction, and sometimes even personnel.

They don't lead with authority. They lead with credibility. If people think they have insight, they do. If their nod means more than a manager's memo, they run the place... without ever saying so.

Guardian Angels or Strategic Roadblock?

Here's the kicker: Shadow Councils are a paradox in motion.

At their best, they're the secret sauce that keeps things running when leadership hits a dead zone. Institutional memory? Check. Mentorship magic? Check. Moral compass during chaos? Double check.

But at their worst?

They're high-functioning neutralizers. They freeze out fresh voices, reward loyalty over ideas, and can twist the truth so smoothly that it starts to feel like fact. They don't argue, they vanish opposition. With a smile.

Why They Thrive in the Fog

Ambiguity is their playground. Matrixed roles, cryptic leadership, and poor communication? That's not dysfunction, it's fertilizer.

Shadow Councils thrive where clarity fails. They read the room before the agenda hits the table. They see what's not being said, and then say it in the right ear.

And even the well-meaning get pulled in. Some become allies. Some become pawns. Most don't even realize they've been drafted.

Night Vision for the Corporate Jungle

Want to thrive where the shadows move? Time to put on your night vision goggles - Enhanced Night Vision Goggle-Binocular (ENVG-B) style. Watch for the signs:

Who gets consulted when no one's watching?

Whose opinion echoes through every "independent" decision?

Who controls the unofficial calendar, or the emotional climate?

These aren't accidents. They're breadcrumbs leading to influence.

Pro tips for navigating the maze:

- Track the patterns. Power doesn't walk in straight lines. It leaves loops and fingerprints.

- Build real relationships. Shadow influencers don't trust slick talk; they rely upon clarity.
- Speak real, but aim well. Loud facts make waves. Smart truth brings change.
- Stay ethical. Influence itself is neutral. Your values decide what it becomes.

The Map Behind the Picture

Although the company has its organizational chart. There is always another map, the one written in innuendo, drawn in glances, and edited during hallway chats.

Shadow Councils don't grab power. They tell their way into it. They decide what matters, what fades, and what becomes the company's next "unofficial" priority.

To ignore them is to miss the real show. To understand them? That's when you stop reacting... and start reading the script before it's written.

So, wondering why decisions feel like déjà vu or why some ideas soar while others sink, don't blame the process.

Just look into the shadows.

The real players are already in motion.

They're not on stage.

Yet, they steal the spotlight.

The Byte House Council of Apple: A Positive Case Study in Hidden Leadership

Welcome back to Apple, circa the 1980s. The surface story? Steve Jobs, turtlenecked, intense, and marching relentlessly toward the future. But just beyond the spotlight, behind a dusty soda machine in a forgotten backroom, real history was quietly being made.

Pull back the curtain. You've just entered The Byte House or The Secret Society of Apple (Its codename)

No official name. No meeting minutes. Just Tuesday nights, dim lights, and a rotating cast of rebels, coders, designers, and what one manager called "too many opinions with no job titles to match." This wasn't a formal task force. This was Apple's Shadow Council.

Leadership Without the Label

There was no hierarchy here. Only influence.

- Woz: The Whisperer. Invented half the tech, but spoke in humility and clarity.

- Susan Kare: The Jester, but not for laughs, her pixel-perfect icons and fonts had punchlines with purpose.

- Rod Holt: The Sheep Dog, absorbing Jobs' impossible demands, shielding the team from firestorms.

- Andy Hertzfeld: The Architect, moving between the technologists and the dreamers with ease.

- Others, nameless to the public, but indispensable in the product.

They weren't at the helm, but they ensured the ones who were didn't crash the ship.

Decision-Making in the Shadows

Jobs would challenge relentlessly, persuade forcefully, and lead with an uncompromising vision, driving teams through scrutiny, inspiration, and a singular focus on simplicity.

The Mac was envisioned to communicate with the elegance and intuition of the future. Its fonts were crafted to evoke the grace and rhythm of poetry, which was refined, expressive, and deeply human. Even its cooling system was designed with intention, operating in near silence to reflect the seamless calm of great engineering.

Official meetings imploded under the constant pressure. But back at The Byte House, the real work began.

Sketches were drawn. The code was hacked. Physics was negotiated, not with memos, but with soldering irons, midnight snacks, and energy drinks.

Chicago. Geneva. Monaco.

Not just fonts. These were quiet rebellions disguised as deliverables. Ideas born in secret, shipped in brilliance.

Jobs took pride. The Byte House took care of Apple.

The Shadow Code of Conduct

There was an unspoken rule: no backstabbing, no politics.

The team understood that if they turned into a closed circle of power, they would become the very problem they aimed to solve.

So, they crafted an invisible code of conduct, never formalized, but deeply felt:

- Ideas mattered more than egos.
- Silence was not disengagement; it was a sign of alignment.
- Leadership was encouraged, but not at the cost of the product.

The Byte House: Apple's Unofficial Operating System

This group never appeared on an organizational chart. Yet it acted as Apple's immune system, filtering erratic input, distilling clarity, and preserving the core of innovation.

They shielded the process from chaos.

They translated ambitious visions into tangible outcomes.

They made sure creativity remained productive, not destructive.

Their influence was never loud. It was exercised through timing, subtle redirection, and collaboration so seamless it seemed predestined.

Legacy of the Invisible

When the Mac was launched, the world celebrated the face of the product. But behind each breakthrough stood a group of individuals who chose to remain in the shadows.

They weren't interested in applause. Their loyalty was to the craft.

Their power lay in shaping the outcome, without claiming the spotlight.

This is the paradox of shadow leadership:

Holding sway without seeking recognition.

Making history while letting others tell the story.

The Byte House wasn't just a clubhouse for code-slinging misfits; it was a containment zone for creative chaos. A place where wild ideas were welcomed, and wilder personalities were quietly course-corrected. Think of it as a behavioural buffer for a certain mercurial visionary with a turtleneck and a temper.

Jobs may have been the face, but the Council was the pulse. He hurled visions like lightning bolts; they caught them, grounded them, and wired them into something that actually worked. He pushed boundaries, sometimes off cliffs. They built bridges mid-fall. It wasn't obedience, it was orchestration. Controlled disobedience in the name of the product.

This wasn't a team that needed hand-holding. They could code blindfolded and debug in their sleep. But even the best systems suffer from noise, misalignments, ego drift, and the occasional personality crash. The Byte House was the self-correcting mechanism, quietly snapping things back into place before anyone outside noticed.

And when the Mac debuted, the headlines sang the gospel of Jobs. Genius. Iconoclast. Lone visionary. The Council didn't mind. That was the job. Influence without spotlight. Power without the podium. After all, shadow leadership doesn't show up in photos, but it always shows up in the product.

So, What's the Lesson Here?

The real structure of a company isn't confined to the hierarchy. It lives in murmured conversations, after-hours alignments, and the quiet confidence of those who build without broadcasting.

The Byte House offers timeless reminders:

- Influence doesn't depend on authority.
- Quiet work can create the loudest impact.
- Real leadership often chooses silence over spectacle.

So next time a bold product or powerful decision captures your attention, look beyond the headlines.

Somewhere, perhaps near a forgotten vending machine, is the room where the future is being quietly rewritten.

The Risks of Shadow Governance

In the corporate village, not all power wears a suit. Some of it lingers in the background, slipping through private chats, forming quietly in break rooms, and shaping decisions far from meeting agendas. This isn't about any formal team or title. It's about *shadow governance*: sometimes a proletariat or bureaucracy of influence that can run beneath even the most well-structured organizations.

Let's be clear, this isn't a critique of stable, transparent leadership groups that help steer the company forward. Every healthy organization needs them. This is about when influence begins to drift away from the light, operating through closed circles and informal alliances that aren't accountable to the broader team.

Think of it as the corporate version of a werewolf: not monstrous, but shape-shifting and hard to spot. It thrives on exclusivity and loyalty, personal power, and leverage not to the company's mission, but to itself. It often bypasses formal channels, making key decisions in side conversations, private messages, or selective social circles.

The shadow councils are often packed with talent, software engineers, product wizards, subject matter experts, and more. And while their intentions are usually golden, over time, they can start to resemble a well-meaning traffic jam.

Why? Because despite their brilliance, shadow councils often lack the big-picture umbrella view, the strategic radar that keeps everyone aiming for maximum impact. They're smart, sure, but sometimes they're playing chess without seeing the whole board.

In such environments, talent alone isn't enough. You could be high-performing, full of ideas, and deeply aligned with company values, but if you're not part of the inner circle, you're left on the outside. That's where culture can fracture. Not because of any one person or team, but because power is being held and exercised without clarity, accountability, or effective communication.

Now, enter the Silos of Expertise.

Imagine a quirky village where teams live like characters in a werewolf game, everyone has a role, and nobody fully trusts the mayor (aka the CEO).

Those laser-focused corporate support functions, such as Legal, Quality, Regulatory, Compliance, Finance, HR, IT, Communications, and sometimes Procurement, particularly those laser-focused on the regulatory pathway, don't sway just because marketing wants a unicorn on the homepage. Nope. They stick to the rules...their rules, protect the mission, and ensure things don't go off the rails.

Here's the twist: building these aligned, self-contained silos *on purpose* (yes, on purpose!) can actually counterbalance the sneaky groupthink of shadow councils. When teams are clear on their purpose, even if they're not all marching to the same drum, they help maintain integrity, clarity, and accountability across the organization.

In short, let the shadow councils brainstorm, but let the werewolf villagers keep to a defined map.

So let's not mistake the presence of leadership for the presence of fairness. Let's call out the real risk: not structured influence, but unchecked, unofficial power that works in the shadows and slowly erodes trust.

How Do You Know a Werewolf Is Lurking?

Watch for These Clues:

1. Decisions Are Made Before Meetings Begin

If every meeting feels like a bad play where the ending is obvious, there's a shadow council backstage calling the shots.

2. A Select Few Always Have Leadership's Ear

If the same two or three people always seem to "have a word with the boss" and mysteriously get what they want, then it's a - ding ding ding!

The truth is, promotions are awarded to those who have the greatest visibility. Ensuring that your work and leadership are recognized by key decision-makers is the most effective way to climb the corporate ladder. Great work that stays in the shadows often goes unnoticed or, worse, can be taken by those in higher positions and presented as their own. Visibility decides promotion, shadow councils, and Werewolf leaders control opportunity and visibility.

3. Whisper Networks Control

If climbing the ladder depends more on alliances than achievements, chances are the werewolf pack is picking who gets to rise. The reality is that promotions often favor those who maintain the greatest visibility within the organization. To ascend the corporate ladder, it's essential to ensure that your contributions and leadership are recognized by those in power. Exceptional work that goes unnoticed risks becoming irrelevant, or, even worse, being appropriated by your superiors and presented as their own achievements. Visibility is key to ensuring your efforts receive the recognition they deserve.

When this hidden council runs the show, the office becomes less like a team and more like a political thriller, minus the fun soundtrack. It's not about skill anymore; it's about survival. About staying close to power. About playing the game when no one gave you the rulebook.

And Where's the HR in All This?

The HR Paradox: Shield or Sword?

Human Resources is often seen as the corporate village's counselor, approachable, empathetic, and committed to employee well-being. But beneath this friendly exterior lies a more complex role. HR departments are not just employee advocates; they are also guardians of the organization's legal, reputational, and financial health. This dual mandate, to support the individual while protecting the institution, creates a tension that is both unavoidable and often misunderstood.

At their best, HR professionals walk a tightrope with grace. They offer a listening ear to distressed employees while quietly mitigating risks behind the scenes. They champion inclusion, fair treatment, and development while also preparing for litigation, policy violations, and performance management. They know the backstories that never reach the surface, the complaints quietly resolved, the red flags raised too late, the toxic managers who survive reshuffles not because they're liked, but because they deliver results.

But here's the uncomfortable truth: HR is not neutral ground. It exists within the power structure of the company. When employees walk into HR to report toxic behavior, they often believe they are confiding in a therapist. But the HR professional is not a therapist; they are a risk assessor, a compliance agent, and a record-keeper. And while many genuinely care, their loyalty is ultimately bound to the organization that pays them.

This is where the Werewolf Paradox rears its head again. HR must investigate the "bite marks" without upsetting the pack. When a powerful manager or senior leader is accused of toxic behavior, HR often finds itself in a triangular trap:

Here are the 3 elements in the triangular trap:

- Support the victim and risk retaliation from leadership.
- Side with leadership and risk losing employee trust.
- Or delay action, hoping the issue resolves itself, only to watch morale quietly corrode from within.

And what of the whistleblower? Once someone steps forward, they are never unseen again. Even if protected by policy, they may face the invisible penalty: fewer promotions, social distance, and being labeled “not a team player.” HR knows this risk intimately. That’s why some departments focus more on plausible deniability than on decisive action.

Yet not all is lost. There is a new breed of HR emerging, what we might call Lunar HR Leaders, those who acknowledge the shadows but still work in the light. They challenge toxic systems from within, quietly reshaping policies, holding courageous conversations, and crafting safer cultures one decision at a time. They know the true cost of inaction, and they choose the harder road when needed.

In a corporate world full of Werewolves, HR can be the healer or the handler. The question isn’t whether they should serve both the employee and the enterprise. It’s how courageously they can do both, and what they risk when they don’t.

Sometimes, the top leader is unaware, blissfully ignorant as the shadows grow stronger. Other times? They know and shrug it off as “just how things work.” Either way, the result is the same: trust erodes, morale crashes, and your best people start updating their LinkedIn profiles.

When employees realize they’re not playing on a level field, motivation doesn’t just dip; it vanishes. Innovation? Suffocated. Collaboration? Poisoned by paranoia. You get a workplace where people insinuate more than they speak, and decisions feel like déjà vu.

So What's the Real Cost?

Shadow governance doesn't just stifle growth; it also breeds fear, favoritism, and frustration. It replaces fairness with politics and potential with protectionism. You end up with a company that looks stable on the outside, but inside? It's a ticking time bomb wrapped in a dress code.

Silver Bullet? Transparency.

If you want to keep the corporate werewolves at bay, put some daylight on everything.

Let decision-making be more visible. Make room for diverse voices, not just the usual suspects. Encourage merit, not manipulation.

Because the best kind of governance doesn't hum, doesn't hide, and definitely doesn't wait for a full moon to show up.

So, the next time you sense something moving in the shadows, just pause. Listen. Look around.

And ask yourself: Is that just the AC kicking in... or did the room suddenly get colder for another reason?

The Asymmetry of Age: Bright Ideas Below, Big Decisions Above

Step inside Synergon Corp, a glass-and-steel mirage of modernity, where every quarter begins with the same ritual: The Strategy Summit - vision decks, buzzwords, breakout rooms.

To outsiders, it looks like collaboration.

To insiders, it's the Werewolf game in a business suit.

Everyone has a role.

Not everybody knows who calls the shots.

Welcome to Age Discrimination - Unspoken, Unwritten, Unmissable

On one side, the Young Wolves. Fresh out of top B-schools, fueled by caffeine and disruption manifestos. They speak in agile sprints, build MVPs overnight, and keep WhatsApp lit into the early hours. They dream, build, and pitch.

On the other side, the Alpha Wolves. Corporate veterans with seasoned instincts and sharper veto power. They've outlasted five CEOs, ten market pivots, and can kill an idea with one well-timed, "Let's revisit this next quarter."

But not all Alpha Wolves howl down ideas. Some teach flight.

She never said much in meetings but made a few quiet calls that saved more than one Alpha Wolf from getting burned. She didn't chase trends but spotted talent before it shone. A wise Alpha Wolf, not feared, but followed.

Yet there's another kind of Wolf - the Grey Wolf, who didn't make it to the C-suite.

And when an Alpha Wolf becomes a Grey Wolf and doesn't make it to the C-suite, what happens? The game changes.

Suddenly, they're no longer on the invite list for key negotiations, and their years of experience and knowledge are undervalued. Their approvals become optional. Their inboxes are quieter. The leadership torch is handed not down, but over to younger, inexperienced managers, in an effort to highlight the newest "high potential".

They're not asked to leave.

They just stop being asked altogether.

Some Grey Wolves don't leave, but they no longer lead either.

You'll find them in the quiet corners, subtly left outside of the decision-making process. Once bold disruptors, now gently faded into irrelevance. Their ideas are still sharp, their loyalty intact, but their relevance, questioned. Age is never mentioned, but it lingers in the room like a paused conversation or deftly inserted into small talk that sounds more like... "so how many more years do you want to work before you retire?".

When enough of their personal stake is eroded, the system gently squeezes them out. A "company severance', with its obligatory non-compete clause. A quiet goodbye. It lingers like a bad breakup, one that never offered closure, now ghosting you into silence. Your self-worth, bruised. Another door might open, eventually, but the sting of subtle dismissal clings to you like a shadow.

And yet... others adapt still.

The Werewolves.

These players bend the rules, hoard information, and wield it like weapons.

Why do they win? Because in the game of Werewolf, knowledge is power, and silence, a strategy.

They survive by staying unpredictable, by mastering perception.

While C-suite leaders are coached to be nice, transparent, and collaborative, Werewolves thrive in ambiguity. They use diplomacy like a disguise. Their bark becomes their brand. Their bite, rebranded as "decisiveness."

But not all werewolves are villains.

Some are survivors in a rigged game.

The Night Phase: Where Work Happens

The Young Wolves burn the midnight oil, sketching wireframes, tweaking prototypes, eating boiled ramen, and swapping strategy theories over encrypted group chats.

They believe the future is theirs to build.

Fast. Frictionless. Fearless.

Then comes dawn, and with it, the review.

The same decks, now in the hands of remaining Alpha Wolves and Grey Wolves. But their reactions differ.

The Alpha Wolves raise eyebrows.

"Too niche."

"Too soon."

"The board won't get it."

Innovation gets Post-it notes... into oblivion.

The Grey Wolves, who once pitched bolder, riskier bets, now sit back. Not out of disinterest, but because no one really asks them anymore. They see their past lives in these slides, yet their voices are no longer part of the review loop.

Once decision-makers, now dignified spectators.

The younger crowd thinks they're resistant. In truth, they're just disconnected.

They didn't leave the game. The game left them.

The Day Phase: Where Applause Happens

At the all-hands, the slides spin stories of collaboration, innovation, and transformation.

The CEO, camera-ready and silver-templed, channels TED Talk energy:

"We're building a culture of bottom-up change!"

Then Michelle, junior strategist, speaks up. Confident. Data in hand. A gamified finance tool with real traction.

A polite pause.

"Let's form a committee to explore this further," says the SVP, all smiles, no door.

Translation? Nice try.

Applause is timed. Approval is rationed.

And visibility? That's a currency Michelle hasn't earned yet.

By the coffee machine, she sighs to her teammate Adi:

"Feels like we're asked to howl ideas just so they can be hunted at sunrise."

The Accusation Round: Someone Always Pays

When a project falters, someone takes the fall.

Too green.

Too idealistic.

Too fast.

Rarely is it the Alpha Werewolves. Their bad bets are rebranded as "strategic restraint" or "executive oversight."

The Grey Wolves? They don't fall, but they fade.

They've seen this round before. They recognize the ritual. They know when to step back, and when they're being edged out.

They're not invited to the table, but their name still appears on the organizational chart.

Still wise. Still labeled "seasoned," as if age was a seasoning, not a strength.

The sharp edge they once wielded is slowly sheathed, to make room for shinier minds with fresher jargon and newer MBAs.

And as the cycles repeat, they watch from the sidelines, unacknowledged, underutilized, and uninvited.

The Endgame: Rare Evolutions

Not all Wolves get hunted.

Some get outpaced.

The Young Wolves race ahead - fast, curious, relentless.

The Alpha Werewolves stay in control - strategic, composed, and deeply political.

And the Grey Wolves?

They linger in limbo. Experienced, burdened, and boxed out by a system that favors disruption over depth, until they are no longer seen as part of the future.

In the Werewolf Game of the corporate world, information is power, and visibility is survival.

Werewolves, those who master perception, timing, and control the shadows, often rise not because they are right, but because they are ready to do what others won't. They're charming in public, ruthless in private, and never fully seen for what they are.

They win because they know more than others.

Because they hide their claws until it's too late.

Because they play both night and day.

But winning isn't the same as leading.

A young leader must learn to tell the difference.

They will meet Werewolves who win at all costs, and Lunar Leaders who elevate others.

They will be tempted by shortcuts and performance theater.

They may even slip into Werewolf mode themselves, masking ambition as diplomacy, control as collaboration.

But eventually, if they're paying attention, they'll see the cost.

Because a system that sidelines experience in favor of speed, or worships disruption while discarding wisdom, is one that eats itself.

The truth? Innovation doesn't wear a name tag. Leadership doesn't come with a birthdate.

Some of the most forward-thinking ideas live in minds with decades behind them.

And some of the most reckless decisions wear fresh sneakers and confidence.

What the corporate world needs isn't younger or older Wolves.

It needs Lunar Leaders who are agile, who adapt, who lead with clarity, no matter what phase of the moon they're in.

The game may never be fair.

But the ones who evolve, not just survive, are the ones who change the rules entirely.

The Truth Beneath the Game

Often, young wolves mimic werewolf behavior early on, manipulation masked as strategy.

But eventually, the good ones understand: It's not the right way to lead.

The real tragedy?

The company splits talent by age:

Young = innovation.

Old = wisdom and decision-making.

But what of those in between?

Middle managers in their 40s and 50s, though strategic and high-performing, find themselves squeezed out of relevance simply for not being disruptive enough or established enough. Too old for the trenches, too young for the throne. They float. Until they're pushed.

What companies fail to see is that innovation is not age-bound.

Nor is stability the sole domain of the grey-templed.

It's not about age, it's about attitude, adaptability, and awareness.

The young brought ideas. The old held the keys.

Until one of them returned, holding both.

And that's when the rules changed.

Loosening the Grip of Unofficial Power

Every company has two organizational charts. One is printed, the other a murmured blueprint. The second is drawn in who grabs lunch together, who syncs at odd hours, and whose quiet nod seems to shift the course of decisions. It doesn't show up in the onboarding manual, but it runs parallel to every meeting and milestone.

These informal power hubs are what we call Shadow Councils. While they might sound mysterious or even harmless, they often shape the true direction of your organization, for better or worse.

Sometimes, shadow councils start off with noble intentions, like secret superheroes lurking in the organizational shadows, capes flapping, ready to *save the day.* They care, they act, they *mean well.* But here's the twist: their vision is often limited to just the slice of the company pie they've been handed. And while they might think they're baking the perfect cake for everyone, sometimes... they're only working with flour and no clue there's no oven.

Without a broader view or the humility to ask, "Hey, what *don't* we know?" these well-meaning folks can stumble. If they're not careful, not growing, not staying flexible, not checking their own blind spots, they risk falling into rigid routines. Think: a mile-deep rut that only covers an inch of ground. That's not a strategy. That's a trap.

In the end, the very people the company counted on to drive change can end up getting stuck. Or worse, buried in the very structures they were meant to influence.

So, how do you distinguish harmless camaraderie from toxic control? How do you root out manipulative cliques without erasing organic, informal influence?

It starts by breaking the grip of unofficial power and channeling it into the light.

The Light Switch: Strategies for Exposing and Redirecting Shadow Power

1. Encourage Open Dialogue - Build a Safe Arena for Truth

Imagine your workplace is a colosseum.

In one version, only the strongest or most politically skilled dare to step in and speak. On the other hand, everyone's invited, and speaking up doesn't cost you your career.

That's the goal: psychological safety.

- Create forums where ideas (and critiques) can be shared without fear of backlash.
- Encourage honest debates, not echo chambers.
- Train leaders to reward dissent when it's constructive.

If your best ideas are buzzed in private but never spoken aloud in meetings, you've got a visibility problem. And the shadows love that.

2. Distribute Influence Equitably - From Elite Clubs to Collective Wisdom

Shadow Councils often rise because official influence is locked behind closed doors. Promotions are mysterious. Decision-making feels rigged. So people form their own clubs, alliances, and inner circles to survive.

Break this cycle by making influence inclusive.

- Invite diverse voices into strategy conversations, not just those who "always know the right people."
- "Do skip-level meetings," where leaders connect with employees below the managerial level
- Create rotating leadership roles, project-based visibility, and mentorship for overlooked employees.
- Use anonymous feedback and 360° reviews to uncover hidden leaders.

When people see that anyone can influence outcomes through merit, ideas, and integrity, rather than secret alliances, they stop whispering and start building.

3. Hold Leaders Accountable - No More Looking the Other Way

Let's face it: some leaders benefit from Shadow Councils.

These unofficial power structures can serve as comfort zones for insecure managers who fear open challenges. But when loyalty becomes more valuable than capability, the rot begins.

- Set clear values and behavioral expectations for leaders, and enforce them.
- If a senior leader protects their favorite "fixer" even as that person erodes trust, it's time for an intervention.
- Make ethics and transparency part of performance evaluations, not just results.

Courageous leadership means stepping into the mess and fixing what's broken, even when it's uncomfortable.

Reimagining Influence: Don't Kill the Vibe, Elevate It

Let's be clear: informal influence isn't the enemy.

That charismatic mid-level manager who rallies the troops during hard times?

That unofficial mentor everyone turns to?

They're vital to your culture. But left unchecked, informal networks can mutate into gatekeepers of opportunity.

So, don't dismantle them, illuminate them.

- Identify these influencers and formally involve them in mentoring, innovation programs, or cultural initiatives.
- Reward informal leaders who build bridges, not walls.
- Help them transition from gossip networks to visible contributors.

When trust, transparency, and ethical leadership replace secrecy and manipulation, informal influence becomes a superpower, not a saboteur.

Growing From Shadows to Spotlight

Shadow Councils thrive in organizations where fear, favoritism, and fog reign.

But the antidote isn't paranoia, it's participation.

It's creating a culture where power isn't passed in hushed tones but earned through clarity, consistency, and courage.

So flip the lights on.

Let influence walk through the front door.

And let your organization become a place where everyone knows how to contribute, and no one needs a secret handshake to do it.

The Path to Ethical Leadership: Moonlight Over Machiavelli

Whether it's a sprawling tech empire, a buzzing startup, or a sleepy local council, in every system, there are two moons that rise when the sun sets: one lights the path forward, the other casts shadows long and deep.

Let's meet our two nightwalkers: the Lunar Leader and the Shadow Operator. Together, they prowl the veil between moonlight and mystery, where logic bends and instincts rule.

The Lunar Leader isn't always the one with the corner office or the official title. Sometimes, they're that quiet analyst who rallies the team to rethink a broken process. Or the product manager who, without fanfare, sparks a collaboration between siloed teams. They don't issue orders; they build alignment. They don't demand loyalty; they earn trust. Like the moon that lights your path without blinding you, they lead without ego, offering clarity in the darkness.

Then there's the Shadow Operator.

They, too, are influential, but like a whisper in a dark corridor. They pull strings from behind the curtain, thrive in the unknown, and feed on confusion. Need to know something? They already knew. Want to suggest a new idea? They'll claim it as theirs tomorrow. The Shadow Operator doesn't build; they scheme. And while they may seem effective in the short term, their power is parasitic. They don't light the way; they steal the light and claim they invented the moon.

So, what's the difference between these two lunar figures?

Intent.

The Lunar Leader wants to lift.

The Shadow Operator intends to leverage.

One creates ripples of empowerment.

The other? Circles of dependence.

One opens doors.

The other locks them from the inside.

Ethical leadership isn't just about being in power; it's about how you use it when no one's watching. It's about standing in the moonlight and saying, "Follow me, let's find the path together," rather than lurking in the shadows and saying, "Follow me... but don't ask too many questions."

It's easy to be fascinated by results. The Shadow Operator often delivers, at first. But behind every sudden success story born in secrecy lies a rotting foundation. Because true leadership doesn't whisper, it resonates. It doesn't plot, it shares.

So if you find yourself rising in influence without a title, ask yourself:

Are you lighting the path, or lengthening the shadows?

Because at the end of the day, the village doesn't remember who filled the room. It remembers who lit it up.

In the next chapter, we'll journey deeper into the village and confront those that roam freely when fear rules the land. Discover The Fear Economy, where werewolves walk in meetings and the howls of chaos are often disguised as "just being realistic."

Chapter 4 - The Fear Economy

We spoke, but silence had the floor.

We nodded, compliance, nothing more.

The cost of truth too high to pay,

So, fear accrued, and courage decayed.

In every meeting room where tension hums beneath the air conditioning, and every boardroom where agendas trump authenticity, there exists an invisible force. It's not anger, nor fear, but something far more insidious, agreement without thought. A silent nod, a forced smile, a half-hearted "yes"- these are the bricks with which echo chambers are built.

It starts innocently. A well-liked leader proposes an idea. Perhaps it's bold, perhaps it isn't. A few enthusiastic followers nod, offering praise, not because the idea is great, but because the speaker is powerful. Others in the room, unsure or skeptical, glance around. They see the nods, feel the current of conformity, and suppress their doubts. A few hold their tongue for fear of seeming negative, or worse, disloyal. By the end of the meeting, the room is unanimous. But the agreement is an illusion. Truth never stood a chance.

In a game like Werewolf, villagers often fall prey to those hiding in plain sight, leaders of chaos cloaked in trust. In organizations, the werewolf isn't always a person. It is sometimes a phenomenon of uncritical agreement, of silence mistaken for consensus. It thrives on the conformity of fear, fear of being wrong, of standing out, of being sidelined. And it kills innovation, one agreeable moment at a time.

The Dangers of Reflexive Agreement

Leadership rooted in fear doesn't always roar; sometimes, it whispers comfort in the form of conformity. It creates environments where employees learn that it's safer to align than to question. This isn't just a matter of culture; it's cognitive programming.

Social psychologist Solomon Asch once demonstrated this through a simple but powerful experiment. Participants were asked to judge the length of lines on cards. When actors in the room deliberately gave the wrong answers, real participants, despite knowing the correct answer, often conformed. The fear of standing out, of breaking from the group, overpowered their certainty.

Now imagine this not in a lab, but in a leadership meeting. A product is clearly failing in beta testing. An employee sees the red flags but says nothing. Why? Because last week, another colleague raised concerns and was subtly reprimanded, their tone was called "negative," and their attitude was "not aligned with the team." The message is received loud and clear. And just like that, another voice vanishes into the silence of a sunk cost fallacy.

Automatic agreement isn't just a lack of resistance; it's the erosion of critical thinking. It allows flawed decisions to go unchallenged. And when everyone agrees, no one grows.

The Mechanics of Groupthink

The term *groupthink* was coined by psychologist Irving Janis to describe a psychological phenomenon where the desire for harmony or conformity in a group results in irrational or dysfunctional decision-making outcomes. It's a slow descent into sameness, where dissent is stifled, alternatives ignored, and criticism perceived as betrayal.

Groupthink is especially dangerous in leadership teams. These are the places where decisions about vision, strategy, people, and future investments are made. And yet, paradoxically, these are often the most risk-averse rooms, places where reputations are protected more fiercely than ideas.

Let's break down the most common symptoms of groupthink in leadership circles:

- Illusion of invulnerability: Teams believe they can't fail because they haven't in the past. This overconfidence leads to risky decisions taken with little analysis.

- Collective rationalization: Warnings are downplayed. Disconfirming evidence is rationalized away as irrelevant.

- Belief in inherent morality: The team believes its purpose is so noble that the ends justify any means.

- Stereotyping outsiders: Critics are labeled as disloyal, negative, or "not a cultural fit."

- Direct pressure on dissenters: Those who voice objections are subtly or openly pressured to conform.

- Self-censorship: Team members with doubts withhold their opinions to avoid conflict.

- Illusion of unanimity: Silence is interpreted as agreement.

- Mindguards: Some members take it upon themselves to shield the group from dissenting opinions.

Groupthink creates a psychological loop, a feedback system where only supportive voices are heard, which reinforces the belief that the group is right. The team becomes its own audience, its own judge, and its own prison.

Common Enablers of Groupthink

But why do echo chambers and groupthink take root so easily in modern organizations?

1. Lack of Experience Diversity in Leadership

Homogeneity in leadership, whether in gender, background, thought, or experience, feeds into similarity of opinion. When leaders come from similar schools, networks, and mindsets, disagreement becomes not only rare but culturally uncomfortable. There is safety in sameness, but also stagnation.

2. Distance to Power

In many corporate structures, hierarchy is treated like sacred geometry. The higher up someone sits, the less likely they are to be questioned. This is especially true in cultures where respect for seniority outweighs the merit of ideas. As a result, employees speak *to please*, not *to challenge.*

When a CEO's joke gets louder laughs than it deserves, that's power distance at play. It's not that the joke is funnier. It's that disagreement that is dangerous.

3. Performance-Driven Conformity

High-performing teams often hide dysfunction behind results. "We're winning, so we must be doing it right." This mindset is dangerous because it suppresses early signs of trouble. When KPIs become shields against criticism, feedback is seen as sabotage rather than support.

In these environments, people don't just conform; they internalise the belief that conformity is excellence. And that's when truth truly dies.

The Werewolf Within

In the Werewolf game, the danger lies not in knowing who the Werewolf is, but in not knowing what questions to ask. The same applies to organizations trapped in echo chambers. Often, the toxic leader doesn't even know they've become the source of silence. They may see loyalty, but it's really fear. They may hear agreement, but it's really resignation.

That's the cruel irony of unchecked leadership influence: the very traits that brought a leader success, decisiveness, confidence, and charisma, become the weapons of dysfunction when left unchallenged. They become the Werewolf, unaware, cloaked in applause.

But in a healthy team, the Villagers fight back, not with pitchforks, but with questions. With curiosity. With a challenge. With the courage to say, "I see this differently."

The Psychology of Staying Silent

It's tempting to blame people for not speaking up. But silence isn't always cowardice; it's often learned helplessness. When employees have seen their input ignored, dismissed, or punished enough times, they stop trying.

This phenomenon was well studied by psychologist Martin Seligman in his work on learned helplessness. Initially applied to animals that gave up escaping shocks they couldn't avoid, it's been widely adapted to understand human behaviour in high-control systems, like toxic workplaces.

Employees conditioned to expect negative outcomes for dissent will disengage, even when the environment improves. That's the cost of echo chambers: not just poor decisions, but broken spirits.

Shattering the Echo – Rebuilding with Reflection and Resistance

In the game of Werewolf, suspicion is the only defence. Villagers must speak, reason, and deduce to protect themselves from the hidden threats within their circle. The Werewolf wins when conversation dies, when doubt is suppressed, and the quietest player is trusted merely because they aren't loud. In those silent gaps, danger thrives.

Now, imagine the boardroom as a village. The leader, charismatic, decisive, could be a protector, but might also be the silent disruptor. The real tragedy? No one knows. No one questions. Everyone smiles. The game ends, not with a dramatic reveal, but with a quiet collapse. This is how echo chambers operate, not through chaos, but compliance.

To understand how we escape this fate, we must first examine how it has played out before. One of the clearest illustrations of this dynamic is found in a corporation that once defined its industry: Kodak.

Case Study: Kodak – When the Villagers Stayed Silent

In the 1990s, Kodak wasn't just a photography company; it was the photography company. Their name was synonymous with memories, with film, with cameras. Their market dominance was so absolute that disruption seemed impossible. But behind the dominance was a fatal flaw: they believed their past success ensured their future relevance.

Internally, voices had begun raising alarm bells. Engineers developed the first digital camera prototype in 1975. But leadership, fearing cannibalisation of their lucrative film business, shelved the idea. The Werewolves in this story weren't villains in the traditional sense. They weren't malicious. They were guardians of tradition, protectors of a business model that had served them for decades.

What made it worse was the absence of resistance. Those who saw the digital shift coming were too low on the hierarchy to be heard, or too scared to speak. Mid-level managers, seeing upper leadership's reluctance, mirrored their optimism. Consensus snowballed, not because it was accurate, but because it was safe.

Kodak didn't lose to technology. It lost to its own silence.

In Werewolf terms, the villagers had all the clues, but no one wanted to accuse the smiling neighbor. They played it safe. They avoided confrontation. And when the lights came on, it was too late.

Confirmation Bias – When the Village Leaders Refuse to Listen

Confirmation bias is the human tendency to seek out and favor information that aligns with our existing beliefs. It's why a leader who believes an employee is "difficult" will interpret every assertive comment as aggression. It's why teams will ignore clear signs of market change because they believe they've already "figured it out."

In the game, if a player suspects someone, they begin to twist every action to support that suspicion. A cough becomes a clue. A pause becomes a lie. And ironically, the actual Werewolf could be right in front of them, blending in with agreement and silence.

This exact mechanism plays out in organizations when echo chambers form. Leaders surround themselves with like-minded advisors. Dissent is interpreted as negativity. External market data that challenges internal assumptions is dismissed as outliers. Success stories from different industries are seen as "not applicable to our culture."

Echo chambers don't just repeat the same ideas; they selectively block out anything that threatens the status quo. And over time, the organization becomes more about defending belief than discovering truth.

Breaking the Cycle – Learning to Accuse the Werewolf

In Werewolf, the only path to survival is communication, uncertain, messy, flawed, but honest. The villagers who ask the uncomfortable questions, who challenge silence, who risk being wrong, those are the ones who disrupt the Werewolf's plan.

In organizations, this same spirit must be cultivated. Not recklessness, but structured dissent. Not paranoia, but constructive resistance.

Here's how organizations can begin to shatter the echo and build resilience:

1. Create the Seer's Seat - A Formal Role for Counterpoint and Clarity

Some of the most successful teams assign someone the explicit role of challenger in strategic discussions. This role isn't about derailing plans; it's about ensuring that every major decision has been stress-tested.

This "Lantern Bearer," or Counterpoint Advocate, unlike the random chaos of the Werewolf, is tasked with representing the perspective that's absent. If everyone is optimistic, they ask about failure modes. If the team is focused on speed, they raise ethical concerns. Their purpose is not to win the argument, but to keep the group intellectually honest.

2. Use Anonymous AI Feedback to Surface Truth

Modern leadership teams are increasingly turning to AI-enabled platforms that allow anonymous employee feedback, sentiment analysis, and conversation audits. These tools can detect patterns: overuse of affirming language ("great point," "agreed," "absolutely") or underrepresentation of opposing views.

When digital tools surface signals that no one is raising red flags, that's a clue. Not always of harmony, but of fear.

In Werewolf, anonymous communication would change the game entirely. It would allow honest accusations without immediate social fallout. Similarly, in the workplace, anonymity gives voice to the hesitant, the junior, the previously burned.

3. Reward Constructive Dissent, Not Just Agreement

Leaders often say, "We're open to feedback," but their reactions tell a different story. A raised eyebrow, a defensive comment, a subtle cold shoulder, all of these teach the team how safe it really is to disagree.

Organizations serious about breaking echo chambers must incentivize dissent. Publicly celebrate those who challenged assumptions. Promote people who show intellectual courage, not just execution speed. Introduce 360-degree reviews that score leaders not on loyalty, but on how often and how well they were constructively challenged.

If Werewolf rewarded villagers for calling out danger, even falsely, the game dynamic would shift. In organizations, this means removing the social cost of being wrong.

4. Bring in External Villagers

Every now and then, organizations need someone from outside the echo chamber to question what's being taken for granted.

Whether it's a consultant, an industry peer, or a rotating shadow board of younger employees, the value lies in fresh eyes. Outsiders don't carry the cultural weight of internal loyalty. They can say, "This doesn't make sense," without fearing political retribution.

In Werewolf, this would be the equivalent of inviting a guest player mid-game, someone who hasn't been emotionally attached to the previous nights' choices and can see with clarity what the villagers have normalized.

5. Create Psychological Safe Zones

Not every battle must be fought in public. Sometimes, employees will only share concerns in safe, small, private conversations. That's not weakness, it's humanity.

Leaders can create "listening zones": one-on-one feedback sessions, closed-door "reverse Q&As" where leadership answers questions without knowing who asked them, or informal forums where junior staff challenge big ideas in a judgment-free setup.

In Werewolf, these side conversations, whispers, and alliances are crucial to detecting the hidden threat. Organizations must not only allow such dialogue but design for it.

Rebuilding the Village: From Fear to Fluency

Breaking an echo chamber isn't about chaos. It's about learning to argue well. It's about moving from silence to signal.

In healthy organizations, villagers don't whisper out of fear. They debate out of trust. They disagree not to destroy, but to defend. They push back not to win, but to protect the future.

And leaders? Leaders stop being the Werewolves, even unknowingly. They stop demanding affirmation and start inviting friction. They ask not "Do you agree?" but "What might I be missing?" They begin to see a challenge not as a threat, but as a trust in action.

Conclusion: Playing to Win, Not Just to Survive

In Werewolf, the quietest player often wins. In business, the quietest team often fails.

The true tragedy of echo chambers is not just poor decisions. It's the lost innovations, the stifled voices, the alternate futures that could've been. But the good news is: games can be replayed. Cultures can be rewritten.

Start by changing the rules. Normalise the challenge. Celebrate the doubter. Listen for dissent. And above all, don't mistake silence for trust.

In the next chapter, we move deeper into the psyche of organizational fear, where control masks as clarity, and leadership becomes less about leading and more about surviving.

The Werewolf may always be among us. But if the villagers keep speaking, keep questioning, and keep listening, we might just win the game.

Chapter 5 - The Illusionists

They walked among us, cloaked in light,
Their tongues of silver smile tight.
A leader, they said, bold and wise,
But all we saw were scripted lies.

No howl was heard, no claw in sight,
Just polished decks and charm at night.
We praised the show, ignored the cost,
And never knew the truth we lost.

For in the game of trust and fear,
The loudest lies are what we cheer.
And when the moon revealed its face,
We saw the wolf, but alas, too late.

Illusionist Leaders Among Us

The Werewolf game begins with a lie. Not an overt one, not the kind shouted across the table, but a quiet, strategic concealment. The wolf smiles, nods, and blends in. They practice humility. They offer just enough reason to escape suspicion. And by the time the villagers realize what's happening, it's already too late.

This is not just a game. This is the modern workplace.

In every organisation, there are illusionists, leaders who ascend not by wisdom or delivery, but by optics, misdirection, and the manipulation of perception. They are the corporate equivalent of the Werewolf. Their strength is not in strategy, but in storytelling. Not in alignment, but in audience control.

They don't lead; they enchant.

The illusionist knows how to be what people want to see. In meetings, they echo buzzwords like "transformation," "alignment," and "growth mindset" while subtly avoiding accountability. They master the art of presence, knowing when to speak, when to stay silent, and when to signal false consensus.

And most dangerously, they often believe their own illusion.

Why We Fall for Them: The Power of the Spellcaster

Just like villagers in the game, employees in organizations want to be trusted. We're wired to follow confidence, especially when wrapped in the aesthetic of leadership: polished speeches, sharp dressing, fast thinking. These illusionists exploit a psychological shortcut known as the halo effect, where one admirable trait, like charisma or eloquence, causes us to assume excellence in all areas.

In Werewolf, the quiet, unassuming player rarely gets targeted in the first few rounds. They "seem nice." They "don't look dangerous." But that's exactly the point, the Werewolf doesn't roar until it's safe.

Similarly, illusionist leaders don't push agendas directly. They float ideas like smoke, allow others to grab onto them, and then act as if the direction was collective. They aren't loud; they are strategic whisperers.

They present data in grand decks, but those decks are full of motion, not movement. Animations over analysis. Phrases like "we're tracking positively" instead of specifics. Their brilliance is not in lying, but in never needing to tell the full truth.

The Charm of the Illusionists

In the Werewolf game, the Alpha Werewolf is often the strongest manipulator. They lead suspicion toward others. They make bold, passionate speeches against innocent villagers. They inject certainty where doubt should be.

In organizations, the illusionist leader behaves exactly the same. Consider:

- They orchestrate all-hands meetings with grand declarations about the future but provide no real metrics.
- They redirect blame using corporate euphemisms: "We missed the target due to macroeconomic headwinds" (translation: we failed).
- They celebrate "collaboration" but make unilateral decisions behind closed doors.

This performance lulls the organization into passivity. Much like in the game, villagers start echoing the Werewolf's suspicions, not because they believe, but because it's safer to align.

And over time, a kind of corporate hypnosis sets in.

People stop questioning. They nod in meetings, privately whispering doubts but never voicing them. Just like villagers afraid to call out the Werewolf for fear of being wrong, employees choose silence over visibility.

And the illusionist grows stronger.

Types of Illusionist Leaders – Werewolves in Different Cloaks

Not all illusionists are the same. Some are cunning tacticians, while others are accidental spellcasters, people who once led with authenticity but slowly got addicted to applause. Here are the common Werewolf archetypes in the workplace:

1. **The Performer**
    - Lives for the stage. Loves Town Halls. Speaks in metaphors and "vision" but avoids the operational grind.
    - In Werewolf terms, the one who talks the most but never gives away any role.

2. **The Chameleon**
    - Tells every stakeholder what they want to hear. In a room of execs, they're strategic. In a room of juniors, they're humble.

- In the game: A player who nods, laughs, and never takes a stand.

3. **The Opportunist**

    - Uses crises to centralize power. When things go wrong, they rise not to solve, but to seize.
    - In Werewolf: The player who steps into leadership "for the good of the village," only to mislead.

4. **The Martyr**

    - Silences dissent not with force, but with guilt. Frames questions as betrayal.
    - In Werewolf: The one who says, "How dare you suspect me? After all I've done for the village?"

Each of these leaders survives through emotional manipulation. Their greatest trick isn't deception, it's social conditioning. They make it harder to speak up than to stay silent.

The Culture That Enables Them

The Werewolf can't win without a silent village. And the illusionist leader can't thrive without a culture that enables illusion.

How does this happen?

- Fear of Consequences: Questioning a charismatic leader is risky, socially, politically, and sometimes even economically.

- Over Reliance on Optics: Promotions go to those who "present well," not necessarily those who lead well.

- Narrative-Driven Cultures: Organizations obsessed with "telling the story" Over fixing the reality create fertile ground for illusionists.

- Passive Middle Management: When mid-level leaders mimic senior illusionists rather than challenge them, the spell deepens.

In these conditions, illusionists are seen not just as safe, they're seen as aspirational.

And that's when the transformation completes. The village isn't just silent. It becomes loyal to the wolf.

Why the Spell Works So Well

Psychologically, humans crave certainty. In ambiguous environments, we look to strong signals for direction. Illusionists provide that, even if it's false.

They speak with clarity in chaos.

They offer momentum when others freeze.

They radiate energy, even if it's not real.

And when paired with corporate theatre, high-production events, slogans, and internal branding, the illusion becomes harder to break. Employees start internalizing the story. They say things like:

- "At least they're confident."
- "They have a plan."
- "Better than indecision."

This is not trust. This is surrender.

It's the same feeling when, in the Werewolf game, someone accuses the wrong player with conviction. The village nods. It's easier to go along than to dissent, because if they're wrong, at least they weren't the only ones.

The Moment of Revelation: Too Late?

In the game, the truth only emerges when the Werewolf is revealed, when a trusted player is suddenly "out", and the village realizes they were fooled all along.

In business, these moments come painfully:

- A failed product launch after millions in marketing
- A massive layoff after years of false growth metrics

- A scandal involving someone who was once celebrated as a visionary

The illusion shatters. People say, "We should've seen it coming." Some did. But the village wasn't ready to listen.

Because breaking the spell requires risk, and most systems are designed to reward stability, not truth.

Setting the Stage for Disillusionment

The goal of this section isn't just to describe the illusionist. It's to hold up a mirror.

Every leader has the potential to become one. Every team can become a village that silences its own best voices.

And just as the Werewolf game becomes thrilling when villagers start working together, businesses become resilient when teams value dissent, question narratives, and demand clarity over charisma.

In the next section, we step behind the curtain. We look at the tactics that illusionists use, the spells they cast, the games they play, and the weapons they wield. And we begin the process of learning how to break the enchantment.

Because the wolf is still smiling.

And the village is still asleep.

Behind the Smoke – Spells, Weapons, and Wolves

In the Werewolf game, the second phase is the most dangerous. The villagers have seen a few disappearances. Suspicion brews. But clarity? Still missing. In this fog of uncertainty, the Werewolves operate with even greater skill, tightening their grip while feigning vulnerability.

This is where corporate illusionists thrive.

If Section 1 revealed *who* the illusionists are and *why* we fall for them, this section dives deeper into *how* they operate. Think of this as the part of the game where you finally start tracking patterns, reading body language, remembering who voted for whom, where strategy meets survival.

The illusionists don't lead with clarity; they manipulate the fog. And in that fog, they cast their most powerful spells.

The Floating Goalpost – Success as a Mirage

The first spell is almost poetic in its simplicity: move the goalpost.

In Werewolf, a wolf may say, "We just need to eliminate that one person and everything will fall into place." Once that player is removed and nothing improves, the wolf shrugs and redefines the target. "Actually, maybe *this* person was the real threat." They keep the village in perpetual uncertainty, always chasing ghosts.

In the corporate world, illusionist leaders do the same with performance metrics.

They start with a bold vision: "We'll increase market share by 20% this quarter." But as the numbers wobble and reality sets in, they pivot:

- "It's not about market share; it's about *strategic presence*."
- "Not revenue, but *brand equity*."
- "Not delivery, but *narrative impact*."

They rename failure as progress. They inflate vanity metrics. They invent new KPIs mid-project. The village keeps running. The wolf keeps smiling.

And the spell holds.

The "Corporate Muzzle" – Silencing the Opposition

Every Werewolf game has a moment where someone dares to speak up. "I think it's her. She's too quiet." But then the accused deflects: "That's personal. Why are you attacking me?" Suddenly, the accuser is the villain. The village recoils.

That's the spellcaster move: weaponizing guilt and emotional framing to shut down dissent.

In business, illusionist leaders do this with disturbing frequency:

- A team member raises a red flag in a meeting. The leader responds, "Are you not aligned with our shared vision?"
- A project manager questions the numbers. The reply: "Let's not be negative when morale is already low."

- A senior stakeholder voices concern. The illusionist says, "This is exactly the resistance that holds us back."

The Werewolf doesn't need to eliminate the villager. They just need the village to turn on them.

Silence follows. Dissent becomes taboo. And truth, now reframed as sabotage, becomes the enemy.

The "Corporate Baton" – The Silent Ritual of Blame

There's a subtle but powerful ritual in both the Werewolf game and the corporate world: the handoff.

In Werewolf, wolves often support each other silently. One wolf takes the fall, but the other stays quiet to maintain the illusion. It's not betrayal, it's a tactic. Sacrifice one, protect the rest.

In companies, this looks like passing the baton of blame.

The illusionist leader, when cornered, doesn't panic. They hand over the project, the team, or the presentation to a subordinate, the "runner." If it fails, the blame falls on that individual. If it succeeds, the illusionist reclaims it in review meetings.

This "corporate baton" is handed off with vague instructions, no resources, and absolute accountability. It's a delegation for disarmament.

The person holding it? Often, someone is promising. Often, someone who believes in the vision. A perfect scapegoat.

The Lead Pipe – Weaponizing the Handoff

Sometimes, the handoff isn't subtle. Sometimes it's designed to break the other person.

This is the Lead Pipe, a poisoned handoff given under the illusion of opportunity. A classic Werewolf move.

In the game, a werewolf might suggest a leadership rotation. "Let's let her lead this round, a fresh perspective." But they already know the vote will go wrong. When it does, the wolf simply says, "She wasn't ready. Unfortunate." The damage is done.

In business, the illusionist might say:

- "Let's have you lead the product relaunch. Great visibility for you."
- "Why don't you present the financials to the board?"

Except the numbers are bad. The strategy is flawed. The illusionist knows it, but steps aside, all smiles.

When it implodes, they re-enter with calm authority, "I should've stepped in earlier. But it's a learning curve."

They appear mature. The scapegoat appears incompetent. And the wolf tightens their grip on the village.

Theranos: The Ultimate Corporate Illusionist

No story illustrates the illusionist better than Elizabeth Holmes and Theranos, a real-life masterclass in corporate deception.

Holmes, with her black turtlenecks and Steve Jobs mystique, cast one of the most powerful spells Silicon Valley had ever seen. She spoke in grand visions: democratizing health care, saving lives, revolutionizing diagnostics.

Her spell was so strong that investors, board members, and even former U.S. Secretaries of State fell for it.

Inside the company, fear ruled. Questioning the tech led to termination. The truth was buried beneath NDAs. The Werewolf didn't just blend in; she became the village's icon.

Her illusion held for nearly a decade. When the full moon came, when facts were undeniable, the village realized how deep the spell had gone.

By then, the damage was global.

Theranos wasn't just a scandal. It was a blueprint: how performance, storytelling, and charisma, when left unchecked, can hollow out even the most promising institutions.

Breaking the Spell: The Rise of the Lunar Leader

So what's the alternative? Who defeats the illusionist?

Enter the Lunar Leader, not the loudest, but the clearest. The one who doesn't perform, but listens. Doesn't dominate, but aligns. In

Werewolf, the Lunar Leader is the player who builds trust quietly, who speaks sparingly but with truth, who calls out patterns without paranoia.

In the organization, the Lunar Leader:

- Defines success transparently, no moving goalposts, and believes clarity is kindness.
- Encourages dissent, even rewards it.
- Refuses to outsource accountability.
- Admits uncertainty instead of faking conviction.

The Lunar Leader knows something the illusionist forgets: light doesn't come from control; it comes from reflection.

Just like the moon doesn't shine on its own but reflects the sun, true leaders don't *generate* trust; they *earn* it, over time, through visibility and humility.

Full Moon Events: Moments of Truth

In the Werewolf game, the full moon reveals everything. In companies, too, Full Moon Events occur:

- A crisis that forces clarity
- A layoff where decisions are scrutinized

- A whistleblower's email
- An audit
- A competitor's leap ahead

These moments either expose illusionists or illuminate true leaders.

A Werewolf panics under moonlight.

A Lunar Leader rises.

Organizations must learn to stage their own full moons, deliberate transparency rituals:

- Reverse town halls, where employees ask and leaders answer
- Open retrospectives of failed projects, often called project autopsies
- "What I got wrong" sessions from leadership
- Anonymous audits of strategy execution

Not to shame. But to reveal.

Because when the village sees clearly, the wolves can't hide.

Moonlight Immunity – Building Cultures that Unmask the Werewolf

In every round of the Werewolf game, one fact remains: the game ends not when the villagers guess, but when they unite.

When suspicions give way to collective clarity, the wolves are outmatched. Not by brute force, but by patterns recognised, questions asked, and silences shattered. This is the moment of moonlight immunity, when the village becomes strong enough to survive the spell.

For organisations plagued by illusionists, this final section offers a roadmap. Because unmasking the wolf isn't about witch hunts. It's about building a system where truth flourishes, where spells fail, and where even the most cunning illusionist can't thrive.

Let's walk through how organizations can *inoculate* themselves, not just from individual wolves, but from the environments that breed them.

1. Rituals of the Moon: Designing Full Moon Moments

In the game, the moon doesn't rise by accident. It's scheduled. It brings light. And it changes everything.

Similarly, organizations need intentional rituals of reflection, Full Moon Moments, that make deception harder to maintain and truth harder to hide.

These aren't once-a-year reviews or sanitized all-hands meetings. These are systemic interventions that pierce illusion.

Examples include:

- Post-Mortems with Teeth: Not just a meeting, but a rigorous, multi-perspective debrief on every major initiative, inviting critics, skeptics, and front-line voices. Illusionists hate these because false narratives collapse under scrutiny.

- Shadow Board Reviews: A parallel leadership structure made up of diverse mid-level talent that reviews strategy and execution. It surfaces insights that the illusionist avoids and empowers villagers with a voice.

- Anonymous Decision Journals: Before major decisions, leaders log their rationale, assumptions, and expectations, not for punishment, but for future accountability. When results differ, the record is reviewed. Did we follow facts or fall for spells?

- Failure Festivals: Public sharing of what leaders got wrong, voluntarily. When top voices admit their mistakes, the illusionist's armour of perfection starts to crack.

Full Moon Moments make truth visible. They don't hunt the wolf; they just remove the fog.

2. Pattern Tracking: The Meta-Game of Werewolf

In Werewolf, skilled players don't rely on gut instinct. They watch. They *track patterns*.

"Who is always silent when we discuss big threats?"

"Who deflects blame subtly but consistently?"

"Who initiates chaos, then fades into the background?"

Organizations can do the same, through structured behavioral audits:

- Repetition Reviews: Is this leader always pivoting strategy mid-way? Do their projects consistently change metrics just before completion?

- Feedback Discrepancy Maps: Compare anonymous upward feedback with public perception. Do their teams feel psychologically safe? Or are they performing alignment while internally dissenting?

- Project Ownership Maps: Who starts things and who finishes them? Are there illusionists who claim credit early and distance themselves late?

This is the meta-game. Not just playing, but understanding *how people play*. It turns suspicion into a system.

3. Spell Disruption: Making Illusions Expensive

Spells only work when unchecked. To break them, we must raise the cost of illusion.

Here's how:

- Reward Authenticity Over Optics: If leaders know that admissions of uncertainty or failure boost credibility rather than threaten it, they drop the spell. Create cultures where a "We don't know yet" earns applause, not punishment.

- Incentivise Dissent: Every wolf fears the villager who speaks up. Flip the power dynamic. Publicly recognize those who challenge groupthink constructively. Give promotions not just for success, but for truth-telling under pressure.

- Make Success Transparent: Illusionists rely on ambiguity. Break it with open dashboards, public OKRs, and visible progress metrics. When success is visible to all, it can't be fabricated.

- Rotate Authority: Power without expiration creates shadow kingdoms. Build in time-bound leadership roles, rotating facilitation in meetings, and peer-led strategy days. It dilutes the spellcaster's aura.

The key is this: illusion thrives in opacity. Bring in the light.

4. Unmasking Without Burning: The Ethics of Exposure

Let's be clear: not every illusionist is malicious. Some start with good intentions, lose their way, and get trapped in their own myth. When moonlight hits, we must reveal, not destroy.

Here's how to do it ethically:

- Private Recalibration Before Public Reckoning: Offer illusionist leaders a structured debrief. Invite them into truth, gently. Show patterns. Ask questions. Most won't change, but some might.

- Narrative Shifts Over Personal Attacks: In internal comms, avoid "X did this wrong." Focus instead on "We learned this. Here's how we're adjusting." Frame the change, not the person.

- Exit with Grace When Needed: If the illusionist won't recalibrate, help them exit without fire. Why? Because how you handle one wolf affects how safe the entire village feels.

Remember: the goal is healing the culture, not feeding revenge.

5. From Werewolf Hunters to Torch Bearers: Cultivating Lunar Leaders

We've talked enough about werewolves.

Let's talk about Lunar Leaders, those rare individuals who radiate clarity.

They're not born. They're made. And organizations can build more of them.

Traits to look for and nurture:

- Reflective Intelligence: They ask, "What am I missing?" before saying, "Here's what to do."
- Courageous Listening: They let others speak first, even when it's uncomfortable.
- Disruption With Care: They challenge the status quo without shaming the past.
- Signal Amplification: They elevate voices that are usually ignored.

Train Lunar Leaders by:

- Embedding ethics in leadership programs
- Coaching on ego deconstruction
- Offering rotations through high-conflict zones, like customer complaints or internal disputes

- Evaluating performance not just by results, but how results were achieved

If werewolves cast spells, Lunar Leaders hold mirrors.

6. The Lunar Calendar: Making Transparency a Rhythm, Not a Reaction

Here's the danger: when the crisis passes, so does urgency.

Illusionist systems creep back in. Spells return.

To stop this, companies must create a Lunar Calendar, a structured cadence of transparency, accountability, and pattern checks. It could look like:

- Quarterly Moon Reports: Anonymous feedback from all levels on leadership effectiveness.

- Biannual Pulse Circles: Cross-departmental meetings where people discuss cultural friction, facilitated, open, and unrecorded.

- Yearly Role Audits: Review power concentrations. Who has too many committees, too much visibility, too little scrutiny?

Make moonlight a ritual, not a reaction.

7. When the Game Changes: Beyond Werewolves and Into Collective Wisdom

Eventually, the village stops fearing wolves.

Because it no longer needs to guess.

It watches.

It listens.

It speaks.

The game changes.

In organisations, this happens when truth becomes cultural oxygen. When every player, regardless of title, feels empowered to name what they see.

It's not about catching the next illusionist.

It's about designing a world where illusion can't take root in the first place.

The Cost of Organizational Self-Deception

Every illusionist leader is a warning.

Each time we allow a spell to go unchecked, we teach the village to distrust truth.

We normalize performance over substance.

We protect charisma more than competence.

We reward storytelling over results.

And we lose good villagers.

We must remember: Werewolves aren't the danger. A silent, passive Village is.

But moonlight changes everything.

So, shine the light.

Name the patterns.

Break the spell.

Because the village deserves to thrive, not survive.

Chapter 6: The Corporate Mirror

A glass that flatters, bends, and lies,
It blinds the heart, it veils the eyes.
It shows the shine, conceals the scar,
A truth distorted from afar.

It echoes back the tale you crave,
A polished mask, a gilded grave.
It hides the cracks, the creeping rot,
Revealing all—except what's not.

But mirrors show the chosen gleam,
A crafted tale, a painted dream.
They hide reality, deny the stain,
Reflecting only what sustains.

The Mirror Effect: Seeing What You Want to See

The most dangerous illusions in business aren't spun by competitors or rivals. They are spun by organizations themselves. A corporate mirror is not a reflection of truth—it's a projection of desire. Leaders, boards, and entire teams begin to see what they *want* to see rather than what *is*.

This blindness is rarely accidental. Risk, dissent, and uncomfortable truths are filtered out, leaving only what sustains the story leaders crave: growth, innovation, and harmony. In this way, companies become trapped not by their enemies but by their own reflection.

The danger of the corporate mirror is not its distortion—it's its seduction. It makes people feel safe in falsehood.

Why Organizations Prefer Illusions

A company that stares too long into its mirror begins to crave flattery over feedback. The shine of quarterly results glosses over crumbling systems. A charismatic leader's vision outshines the quiet voices of warning. Teams cheer success slides while ignoring the rot beneath.

Why? Because illusions are comfortable. They protect fragile egos, sustain boardroom confidence, and keep stock prices afloat. The mirror reassures everyone that the path is straight—even when the ground beneath them shifts.

In Werewolf, villagers fall prey to the same trap. They trust smiles over silence, nods over nuance, and consensus over truth. They don't want to see the wolf, so they squint until the danger looks like a friend.

The Mechanics of the Corporate Mirror

How does this illusion sustain itself? Not by accident, but through carefully engineered reflection.

- **Selective Metrics** – Reports emphasize what is improving and bury what is declining. KPIs are shaped like funhouse glass: stretched in one place, shrunk in another.
- **Optimism Theater** – Leaders reward enthusiasm over candor. Anyone who raises concerns is cast as "negative" or "not a team player."
- **Narrative Control** – Stories are polished before they're told. Failures become "lessons learned." Layoffs become "strategic realignments." Decline becomes "transformation."
- **Echo Chambers** – Over time, only agreeable voices remain in the room. The mirror reflects not reality but consensus—curated and fragile.

What's most frightening is that leaders often believe their own reflection. They aren't lying to others—they're lying to themselves.

Case Study: The Boeing Mirror

Consider the 737 Max crisis at Boeing. For years, the company's reflection was one of engineering excellence and safety. Internally, however, engineers raised red flags about design flaws and cultural decay. But the mirror showed profitability, speed to market, and shareholder return.

When risk was raised, it was reframed. When cracks appeared, they were painted over. The corporate mirror told executives and regulators what they wanted to see—until the truth shattered in tragedy.

The lesson? Mirrors don't protect organizations from reality. They only delay its arrival.

How Mirrors Become Masks

A mirror, at first, is a tool. It helps a company project success to investors, confidence to customers, and unity to employees. But the longer the mirror is used, the more it becomes a mask.

- Leaders begin speaking in polished soundbites rather than honest assessments.
- Teams inflate results because bad news won't be welcomed.
- Cultures grow fragile, unable to withstand contradiction.

At this stage, the mirror no longer reflects anything real. It conceals the scars, denies the stain, and replaces truth with theater.

Mirrors for Hire: The Consultant's

Consultants, at their best, can provide clarity, objectivity, and fresh perspective. But in the wrong hands—or without strong oversight—they can become dangerous mirrors. Instead of revealing reality, they reflect back exactly what leadership expects to see.

The cautionary tale is twofold. First, consultants can become a smoke screen. When a strategy fails or a decision backfires, leadership points to the report: *"We were only following expert advice."* The mirror is broken, but the shards fall elsewhere. The consultant becomes the scapegoat, and the executive image remains polished.

Second, consultants can serve themselves. Many firms have perfected the art of selling the reflection twice—first, the diagnosis of the problem (at a premium), and then the solution to fix it (at an even higher fee). In this arrangement, the mirror isn't just flattering—it's profitable. The organization pays to be told what it already suspects, then pays again to chase the promised cure.

Without strong governance, this cycle can hollow out a company. Internal expertise is sidelined. Employees lose voice and ownership. Leaders begin to confuse invoices for insight. And in the end, what's purchased is not truth but theater—an illusion of progress projected in glossy slide decks.

The danger of the corporate mirror is never just what it hides. It's how much people are willing to pay to keep it polished.

Breaking the Mirror

Every illusion eventually cracks. The question is whether the break happens under leadership's control—or under crisis.

Organizations that survive are those willing to shatter their mirrors before reality does it for them. That requires courage. It requires leaders to ask the questions they don't want answers to:

- What are we not seeing?
- Who have we silenced?
- What risks are we denying because they don't fit the story?

Breaking the mirror is not about pessimism—it's about resilience. Villagers survive in Werewolf not by believing the mirror, but by questioning it. In business, the same holds true.

Beyond The Reflection

The corporate mirror is seductive, but dangerous. Leaders must resist the comfort of flattery and the ease of curated truths. To build organizations that last, they must value what *is* over what looks good, and reward those who reveal cracks instead of those who conceal them.

Because the mirror always flatters—until it doesn't. And when it shatters, the village pays the price.

The Alternative: The Lunar Leader

Where the illusionist hides truth, the Lunar Leader reveals it. They are not afraid of the moonlight; they thrive in it. Lunar Leaders do not fear ambiguity, but they name it. They reward reality, not appearances. They do not sell visions; they build them collectively.

Lunar Leaders are the counterspell. They bring light into every dark corner of the village. And they build trust, not traps.

Full Moon Events: Rituals That Reveal the Truth

You can't wait for an exposé to uncover deception. You must create moments, Full Moon Events, that regularly surface hidden truth:

- Anonymous retrospectives
- Peer reviews across departments
- Ethics councils

- Exit interviews are reviewed publicly

- Culture check-ins with skip-level staff

These rituals ensure that no illusion can live forever.

Summing It Up

Illusionists win when everyone else agrees to keep pretending. When villagers look away. When metrics matter more than meaning. When charisma blinds judgment.

But the Werewolf game always ends the same way: with someone finally pointing and saying, "I see you."

So, raise the lantern. Light the path.
Because no illusion can survive the full moon.

Chapter 7 - Building the Resilient Village

The wolves are gone, but not their mark,
Their echoes haunt the village dark.
Though morning breaks with softer skies,
Old fears still wear a familiar guise.

The chains are snapped, the spell undone,
Yet habit hides from the rising sun.
For not all wounds are made by teeth,
And silence lingers underneath.

So, ask yourself when night has passed:
Will you rebuild, or just outlast?
The game is done, the masks are gone,
Now who will lead when comes the dawn?

The Werewolf game is over.
The night rounds have ended.
The villagers survived.
The wolves, unmasked.

But as anyone who's played the game knows, what comes next is far harder than the game itself. There's no narrator to move the plot forward now. No rules to follow. No singular enemy in the shadows.

Only one question remains: What kind of village do we want to build now?

From Survival to Sovereignty

For chapters now, we've navigated the dark: the illusionists, the fear leaders, the groupthink enablers, the silent bystanders, the scapegoat rituals, and the spellbound organizations.

It has been a journey of detection, of survival, of dodging deception.

But we must now move beyond survival.

Because surviving fear is not the same as leading forward.

Villagers who merely survive the Werewolves may still carry the habits of night: distrust, hierarchy, and secrecy. They may lock their doors even when the sun is high. They may whisper when they should speak courageously. They may repeat the mistakes of the past because the old game, even when deadly, had clear rules.

That's the irony of toxic systems: they are miserable, but they're familiar.

The resilient village must break the cycle.

Not with more fear, or better spells, or smarter guesses.

But with a new kind of leadership, leadership that starts when the Werewolf game ends.

Leadership Begins at Dawn

Think about the game of Werewolf again. At first, it rewards suspicion. You win by catching liars. You win by not trusting too much. You win by doubting.

But this is not leadership. This is defense. This is wariness masquerading as wisdom. Now that the wolves are gone, who teaches the children to play again?

Who helps the scorned to find their voice? Who turns the empty well into a gathering place?

That's the work of leadership. And it begins after the fear.

In organizations, this is the moment when the toxic manager leaves. When the hostile culture is exposed. When the PR crisis forces change. When the illusion cracks.

But too many companies stop there. They think removing the problem is the solution.

They forget:

The absence of a wolf does not make a healthy village. It just creates a vacuum.

And nature, as well as corporate life, abhors a vacuum.

Unless intentional leadership takes its place, a new wolf will rise.

Different shape.

Same bite.

Why Organizations Stay Haunted by Poor Leadership

Why do so many companies, after firing the illusionist or toxic executive, find themselves back in the same place within a year or two?

Because they never left the Werewolf mindset.

They stayed in the loop of reaction:

- "Let's investigate more rigorously."
- "Let's hold someone accountable. Everyone has to be more accountable."
- "Let's restructure."
- "Let's hire a new savior."

What they don't realize is that healing a village is not about hunting better. It's about building stronger.

And that requires a different game entirely.

From Fear Games to Trust Fields

Let's reframe.

If the Werewolf game is a game of survival through suspicion, then building a resilient organization is a game of survival through trust, transparency, and visionary leadership.

In this new game:

- The goal is not to find the liar, but to build truth and feedback systems.
- The players are not enemies, but interdependent agents.
- The reward is not to "win" at someone's expense, but to win with everyone still standing and more resilient.

Leadership in this new village is not about clever strategy. It's about emotional labor, vision alignment, and sustained presence.

It's about showing up after the storm, and saying: "Now, let's decide who we want to become."

Who Leads After the Game Ends?

In the Werewolf game, certain players naturally emerge as loud voices. They dominate discussions, accuse, deflect, lead witch hunts, or call for votes.

But in the post-game world, these same voices are often the least effective leaders.

Because this world demands:

- Listening over telling
- Repairing overreacting
- Patience over pure performance

It needs the Lunar Leaders we met earlier:

- Those who lead with clarity, not just charisma
- Who asks more questions than they answer?
- Who are okay with not being the center of attention
- Who refuses the need for an enemy to justify their purpose?

They are, in a sense, the opposite of the Werewolf archetype.

They don't shape-shift.

They don't howl.

They don't need the cover of darkness to operate.

Their power is quiet but steady, like the moon.

They illuminate.

Not interrogate.

The Village as Metaphor for Culture

In organizational terms, the village is your culture.

It's what people believe is okay to say in a meeting.

It's whether junior employees speak up, empowered.

It's whether exit interviews are honest or guarded.

It's whether success is celebrated when it's collaborative, not just individual.

The resilient village is not afraid of high performance. It simply refuses to trade values for victory.

It doesn't hide feedback.

It doesn't hoard knowledge.

It doesn't create kings and pawns.

In a resilient village:

- The goal isn't to "win the round." It's to build a community that survives all rounds.
- The cost of silence is higher than the cost of disagreement.
- Leadership isn't about declaring safety. It's about designing it into the system.

We Were All Villagers Once

Here's the truth.

We've all been players in the Werewolf game.

We've all, at some point, chosen silence over speaking.

We've all believed the illusionist because it was easier than rocking the boat.

We've all watched someone be thrown out of the village unfairly and thought, "Better them than me."

We were surviving.

But that's not a sin.

The sin is staying there once the game is over. Because the dawn is here now.

And the question is no longer: "Who is the werewolf?"

It's: "Who is willing to build a village worth protecting, even when rebuilding the village takes longer than the average three to five-year CEO contract?"

The Threshold Moment

Every organization, every team, every leader, eventually reaches this threshold moment:

The wolves are gone. The howls are quiet. The night has passed.

Now, the real work begins. This is not the end of the story.

This is the beginning of leadership. Not the kind that makes speeches, but the kind that builds firepits, shares food, gets personal, and teaches others to lead.

This chapter, and this section, begin that journey. Because the village deserves more than survival, it deserves vision. It deserves a voice. It deserves you.

The Unseen Toxins: Why Culture Doesn't Change

In the game of Werewolf, when a wolf is discovered, the village breathes a sigh of relief. One threat down. The suspicion feels justified. The air seems clearer.

But soon, paranoia creeps in again.

A side glance.

A missed cue.

A hesitant vote.

"Wait... what if there's another?"

Even after the wolves are gone, the fear remains.

Even in daylight, people act like it's still night.

This, right here, is the tragedy of most organizations.

They think cultural change is about removing the bad guy. But in reality, it's about unlearning the bad behaviors.

The Game Lingers in Micro-Moments

Once a team has played Werewolf for long enough, literally or metaphorically, it becomes second nature.

You start:

- Withholding thoughts that could make you a target.
- Reading the room for alliances instead of authenticity.
- Interpreting silence as a strategy, not discomfort.

In organizations, this is what we call micro-behaviors, tiny, often unconscious acts that collectively shape culture.

Let's say you've removed the toxic VP.

What remains?

- The intern who learned not to speak unless spoken to.

- The manager who survived by always nodding and constantly measuring for loyalty or false PIPs.
- The HR leader who filed complaints into folders marked "Sensitive: Do Not Pursue."
- The CEO now avoids confrontation for fear of repeating the past.

The wolf may be gone, but the rules of the game have not changed.

The village is still haunted.

Fear Leaves Footprints

One of the cruelest ironies of fear-based leadership is that it rewires people, even after the leader has left.

Here's what that looks like:

- Chronic Caution: Employees double-check every sentence in an email, not for grammar but for political survivability. Micromanagement creates complexity, fear, and failure.

- Ghost Approval: Teams still ask, "Would he have been okay with this?" about someone no longer there.

- Feedback Freezes: Even after open-door policies are introduced, no one walks in, because the memory of slammed doors still echoes.

The organization has become a haunted village. The wolves are gone, but their howls are embedded in the walls.

You can fire a leader, but unless you exorcise the habits, the shadow remains.

Micro-Traumas, Macro Impact, and no, I'm not talking about the catch phrases of victimhood and hurt feelings.

Every toxic culture is built not only by massive betrayals but by thousands of micro-traumas:

- Being interrupted in every meeting. Cut off or dismissed.
- Being praised publicly, but undermined privately.
- Having your data questioned while someone else's gut feeling is trusted.
- Watching promotions go to the loudest, not the most honest

These are not headline scandals. They're background noise.

But together, they create a culture of quiet survival, where everyone's just trying to last another day without getting bitten by the types of change management that never manage to change anything.

It's like the villagers are still playing Werewolf... even though the game ended weeks ago.

The Organizational Immune System

There's a concept in organizational psychology called the immune response. It refers to the organization's ability to reject anything unfamiliar, even if it's healthy.

For example:

- A new manager encourages debate? The team calls them "abrasive."
- A new hire questions old assumptions? They're seen as "not a culture fit."
- HR implements 360-degree feedback? The leadership team dismisses it as "a waste of time."

These are not deliberate attacks. They are cultural antibodies, designed to protect the village, but in doing so, they preserve dysfunction.

The result?

Change is chased out. Truth is sanitized. Progress is politely suffocated.

In the Werewolf game, this is like exiling the only player who spoke the truth because they "seemed suspicious."

In corporate life, this happens every time an honest employee leaves, not because they failed, but because they told the truth too often or ran into a bad case of confirmation bias from a weak, insecure manager.

Why "The Fix" Doesn't Fix It

Many organizations, upon recognizing cultural issues, jump straight to solutions:

- Launch a new DEI initiative.
- Bring in a high-profile consultant.
- Rebrand with new values and glossy posters.
- Host a culture-building offsite with motivational speakers.

All these things have optics. They show movement. They feel like action.

But they don't change behavior.

Because the real problem is still playing out in the meeting room, on the floor, in the casual banter, and in the hiring conversations.

Culture isn't changed by campaigns. It's changed by what is tolerated and rewarded in micro-interactions between leadership stakeholders.

In Werewolf terms, it's not enough to name the werewolf.
You must stop playing like one.

The Quiet Cost of Survival Culture

Let's name the symptoms of a culture that still lives in Werewolf mode:

- Silence Over Substance: Meetings where everyone nods but nothing real is said.
- Fear-Based Follow-Through: People act not because they believe, but because they fear the consequences of inaction.
- Leader Worship: The loudest or most powerful voice dominates, even when they're wrong.
- Ghost Stories: Employees still tell horror tales about the "old boss" or "that team", as if they're cautionary myths, keeping people in line.
- Disengagement Dressed as Compliance: People tick all the boxes but have mentally checked out.

This is not healthy. This is cultural PTSD.

It's the village walking around in daylight, still afraid of shadows.

The Real Fix: Leadership + Accountability + Transparency

Here's where most organizations get it wrong:

They either:

1. Focus on Leadership: Charismatic talks, bold visions, emotional appeals.
2. Focus on Accountability: Metrics, punishments, scorecards.

But the solution is not either. It's both.

You need leaders who are:

- Emotionally intelligent and structurally honest.
- Visionary and willing to be held accountable.
- Empathetic and consistent.

It's not enough to say, "We believe in transparency." You have to make truth-telling a norm, not an exception.

It's not enough to say, "People first." You have to ensure that people who mistreat others, no matter their performance, are called out because People First starts with YOUR PEOPLE.

And perhaps most importantly:

You need to make it safe to admit when you were playing the game, too. Because every leader, no matter how noble, has, at some point, chosen safety over truth.

The key is not perfection. It's willingness to step out of the game and name the rules you once followed.

That's how the village heals.

The Werewolf Reflex: Why It's Hard to Stop

There's one more reason cultures don't change even after the threat is gone. We miss the clarity of enemies.

In the game, the world is simple:

- There are Werewolves.
- There are Villagers.
- We must survive.

It gives purpose. But when the game ends, and no new enemy appears, we start inventing them.

We begin:

- Micromanaging.
- Gossiping.
- Blaming departments instead of dysfunction.

Because we were trained to always be against something.

Leadership is harder when you're not fighting, but building.

It's harder to ask:

- "What's working?"
- "What needs to evolve?"
- "How do we build trust without a common threat?"

But it's also where real progress lies.

The Village Rewrites the Rules

To escape the leftover Werewolf mindset, the village must do something radical:

It must write new rules. Together.

Not slogans. Not HR memos. But lived agreements:

- "We challenge ideas, not people."
- "We reward honesty, even when it's messy."
- "We assume good intent but hold people accountable for impact."
- "We don't need a common enemy to feel like a team."

This is how the village transitions from reacting to fear to responding with strength.

This is how culture becomes a living thing, not a haunted one.

Shedding the Fur

Think of the metaphor: The Werewolf sheds its fur to become human again.

Cultures must do the same.

Shed the defense mechanisms. Shed the paranoia. Shed the survival mode. Shed the habit of waiting for another attack.

And in their place, grow something new:

A leadership culture rooted not in "guarding our own self-interests, but in thriving together through shared growth and achievement."

Because the moon may rise again, but in a resilient village, it brings not fear...but clarity.

Selling Fear: Why Some Wolves Get Promoted

In the world of Werewolf, it is not the most honest who survives; it's often the most persuasive, loud, and strategic. The werewolves, after all, aren't just hiding; they're playing. And the best players know how to speak the language of the village. They don't just blend in. They charm, lead, inspire, and when needed, eliminate threats quietly. They're masters of manipulating perception.

In corporate life, these players are everywhere, in boardrooms, sales war rooms, investor meetings, and town halls. They win applause, awards, and even promotions. They are often called "high performers," and their methods, however questionable, are tolerated, even rewarded. The reason? Because they produce results. And in many organizations, results matter more than respect.

This is how werewolves don't just survive, they climb.

The Performance Paradox: When Results Excuse Behavior

The typical corporate narrative sounds like this: "Yes, she's tough, but she gets things done." Or "He might rub people the wrong way, but his numbers are unbeatable." The underlying message is clear: results justify behavior. Performance is the only currency that counts. And so begins the dangerous illusion that outcomes excuse ethics.

But here's the catch: what looks like strength is often controlled fear. Many "top performers" in sales-driven cultures lead not by trust, but by intimidation. They extract compliance, not commitment. Their teams perform under pressure, not inspiration. Yet because the metrics look good on paper, revenue, churn, acquisition, and expansion, the leadership pipeline mistakes control for capability.

In the Werewolf game, imagine a player who leads the villagers with confidence, directs every vote, and claims every insight. They seem like a hero. But in truth, they're eliminating others strategically, the very wolf they fear is among them. They're just too good at hiding. And everyone's too busy admiring their strategy to question their morality.

This is the Werewolf illusion in leadership, when influence masks intention, and the system falls for charisma over character.

High-Stakes Environments: Breeding Grounds for Werewolves

Not all environments are equally fertile for werewolves. Some, by design, are far more vulnerable to the rise of fear-based leadership. Fast-growing startups, aggressive sales teams, venture-backed firms, and high-pressure consulting cultures are particularly susceptible. Here, the appetite for growth at any cost makes fear a fast fuel.

These cultures glorify hustle. They reward 18-hour days, idolize unicorn valuations, and create narratives of warrior leaders who fight, kill, and win. In such an environment, the village doesn't just tolerate werewolves, it hires them. Intentionally. Because the belief is that nice guys finish last, and that "wolves eat sheep" is not a warning, but a strategy.

The tragedy? These environments often attract passionate, intelligent, and ethical people who genuinely want to contribute. But once inside, they're forced to adapt. They either learn the rules of survival, staying quiet, staying busy, staying visible but not too bold, or they burn out, leave, or worse, mutate.

Yes, mutate.

Many good leaders become wolves by accident, because survival demanded it. Because the system rewarded sharp elbows, louder voices, and cutthroat ambition. Eventually, they become what they once opposed.

This is not a moral failing of the individual. It is a structural problem, a village that teaches everyone that barking louder is the only way to not get bitten.

Uber's Culture: A Case Study in Werewolf Leadership

If ever there was a real-world example of this phenomenon, it was Uber under Travis Kalanick. In its early years, Uber was the poster child of disruption, breaking into markets aggressively, fighting regulators, scaling fast, and shattering every traditional notion of how a transportation business should behave.

Internally, this translated into a culture of unapologetic aggression. Employees were rewarded for "toe-stepping," a euphemism for stepping over others to climb. Managers were expected to defend their turf, not collaborate. Feedback was seen as a weakness. And HR, the traditional protector of employee rights, became a tool for shielding top performers, no matter the complaints against them.

In the Werewolf metaphor, Kalanick was the alpha wolf, not because he was evil, but because the game rewarded him for it. His charm, brilliance, and ruthlessness combined into a character that investors adored and employees feared. The company grew at rocket speed, but so did the body count. From sexual harassment allegations to systemic sexism, from data leaks to a toxic culture of retaliation, the signs were everywhere. But the game didn't stop until the board could no longer ignore the wounds of the village.

And even then, many questioned whether removing Kalanick would change the DNA of Uber's leadership culture. Because while the wolf was gone, his playbook remained.

Why Boards and CEOs Let the Wolves Run Freely

Why do the people at the top, boards, investors, and executive teams allow toxic leadership to fester? The answer lies in short-termism.

Werewolves create the illusion of security and growth. They're assertive, decisive, "in control." They can speak fluently in investor language, dominate earnings calls, and demand loyalty. They look like leadership incarnate.

So, when the board is nervous, the company is bleeding cash, or competition is fierce, fear wins. Boards don't want ethical reform;

they want stability. They want numbers. And wolves deliver numbers, at least temporarily.

It's the equivalent of burning the village to save it.

Eventually, the damage becomes visible, including turnover, lawsuits, press scandals, and employee activism. But by then, the original players are gone. The wolf has moved on, with stock options cashed and a reputation rebranded.

And the village is left to rebuild, confused about how they let it happen, again.

The Villager's Dilemma: Compliance or Courage?

The villagers in Werewolf know one truth: speak too early, and you're voted out. Stay quiet, and maybe you survive.

This is the exact dilemma employees face in fear-based leadership environments. They see what's wrong. They feel the manipulation. They sense the harm. But they stay silent. Because the system punishes whistleblowers and praises team players, even if that "team" is sinking.

Fear doesn't just kill innovation. It erodes morality.

People start justifying bad behavior:

- "Well, at least he's not shouting this week."

- "She only undermines others when her targets are big."
- "It's not my problem; I'm just here to do my job."

The village becomes complicit. Not out of malice, but out of exhaustion. It's hard to fight a wolf when you're trying to feed your family.

So, fear wins. Slowly. Quietly. Efficiently.

The Transformation Begins with the Scorecard

If organizations want to stop promoting wolves, they need to stop counting fangs as features. That begins with changing how success is measured.

Right now, most performance metrics are built around output:

- Revenue
- Market Share
- Margin

- Growth

These are vital, but they don't paint a full picture. We must start asking:

- How was that growth achieved?
- Did people grow under this leader, or just perform?
- What was the turnover in their team?
- What's their 360-degree feedback?

In Werewolf, this is like asking: "Did this player win by helping the village? Or by tricking it?"

Until organizations reward truth over theatrics, they will keep hiring charmers and rewarding manipulators.

Choosing the Lunar Leader Over the Alpha Wolf

There is an alternative archetype, which this book calls the Lunar Leader.

The Lunar Leader isn't loud, but they're clear. They don't silence dissent, they welcome it. They don't lead by fear; they lead with clarity, conviction, and character.

Their power doesn't spike during full moons. It shines broadly every day.

They recognize performance but refuse to trade integrity for quarterly wins. They understand that lasting success is not built by extracting the most out of people but by unlocking the best within them.

They know how to play the game, but they choose not to.

In Werewolf, the Lunar Leader would be the villager or the SEER who, when faced with uncertainty, asks better questions. Who defends the silent. Who delays judgment until they know enough to vote fairly.

They might not always win. But they always protect the integrity of the village.

The Cure for Fear is Courage, Not Compliance

The only thing that breaks the spell of the werewolf is truth, courage, and collective awareness. You can't fight fear with rules. You can't regulate ethics into existence. And you definitely can't hire your way out of cultural decay.

The transformation begins when enough people in the village decide they will no longer play the old game. When they choose to be curious, not compliant. When they choose to lead, not manipulate. When they value trust more than tribal loyalty.

Because leadership is not about surviving the night.

It's about making sure the village never needs to play Werewolf again.

The Five Tenets of the Resilient Village

In the game of Werewolf, one thing is constant: villagers lose when they act in isolation. When each player operates in fear, hoarding suspicion, second-guessing allies, and looking over their shoulder, the werewolves gain power. But when the villagers communicate openly, verify information, and begin to build shared trust, something changes. The fog lifts. Patterns emerge. Wolves get nervous.

This principle is no different in organizations. A toxic leader, the Corporate Werewolf thrives in chaos, thrives in mistrust, thrives in environments where people feel disconnected and disempowered. The moment the culture begins to stitch itself together, to become a resilient village, the manipulation becomes harder. The lies become visible. And the system begins to protect itself.

So, what does it mean to build such a village? It requires commitment to five tenets, foundational principles that create psychological immunity in an organization. These aren't values for a wall. They're not slogans for a website. These are lived truths that must be embedded into every decision, meeting, and leader's behavior.

Let's unpack them through the eyes of the Corporate Village.

Tenet 1: Radical Clarity – The Lantern in the Fog

The first and most essential tenet of a resilient village is clarity. Not partial truth. Not polished spin. Radical clarity. The kind of clarity that refuses to hide behind acronyms, complexity, or performance theater.

In the game of Werewolf, villagers are often destroyed by confusion. They guess at motivations. They speak in hints. No one wants to be the first to call out someone too early. And so, the wolves thrive in the fog. Every vague statement, every half-guess, every silence creates shadows. In those shadows, deception thrives.

In business, this shows up as unclear and unattainable goals, shifting priorities, and veiled communication. Employees don't know what's expected of them. Managers hint at problems but don't coach. Teams smile in public but harbor resentment. Clarity becomes a casualty of corporate diplomacy.

To fight this, resilient villages must light the lantern. Leaders must over-communicate. They must speak the uncomfortable truths. "Here is where we are. Here's what's broken. Here's what's being done." No euphemisms. No PR tone.

Even when clarity is painful, especially when it is, it creates safety. When people know the truth, they can make decisions. When they don't, they operate in fear. Fear, as we know, is a werewolf's favorite weapon.

Tenet 2: Distributed Courage – The Village Doesn't Wait for the Mayor

Courage is often imagined as a leader standing alone at the front, making bold decisions. But in a resilient village, courage isn't a personality trait; it's a shared behavior. Distributed across teams, layers, and functions.

In Werewolf, players often wait for someone else to speak first. "What if I'm wrong?" they ask themselves. "What if calling someone out makes me the next target?" So they stay silent. They wait for the alpha to speak. And usually, the alpha is the werewolf.

Organizations do this too. They rely on senior leadership to drive integrity. But culture isn't built from the top alone. It's built on ion conversations between peers. In moments when someone says, "That's not okay," or "Can you clarify that?" or "I think we need to slow down and assess this decision."

Distributed courage means creating a system where people are rewarded for surfacing the truth, not punished. It means HR that protects people, not power brokers or KPI's. It means town halls that welcome challenge, not staged praise. It means encouraging new employees to question why things are done a certain way, and letting them know their voice matters even before they've earned influence.

A village where only one person is brave is a doomed village. Resilience is built when every villager carries a little torch of truth.

Tenet 3: Restorative Accountability – Not Just Who's to Blame, but What We Learned!

Werewolf is a brutal game. One vote, and a player is eliminated, often without recourse, often based on suspicion. The game doesn't allow second chances. You're either right, or you're gone.

Organizations that mimic this binary thinking create fragile cultures. People fear mistakes. They hide failures. They point fingers to protect themselves. Leaders punish publicly to "send a message." But all this does is train villagers to play safe, lie low, and never take bold steps.

Resilient villages practice restorative accountability. This means that when something goes wrong, the question isn't just "Who failed?" but "What failed in our system that allowed this?"

Accountability isn't scapegoating. It's a reflection. It's rebuilding. It's an honest debrief followed by constructive repair.

Yes, people must be held responsible. But the goal isn't shame. The goal is learning. The best leaders don't eliminate players who get it wrong. They invite them to examine the misstep and improve the rules for everyone.

Werewolves hate this. Why? Because it breaks the drama. It reduces fear. It replaces performance with process. And wolves, remember, only win when the village turns on itself.

Tenet 4: Inclusion as Defense – When Every Voice Counts, Lies Get Louder

One of the most powerful tools in Werewolf is groupthink. Wolves know that if they can manipulate a few loud voices, the rest will fall in line. Exclusion isn't just discrimination; it's a strategy. The fewer voices that speak, the easier it is to control the story.

In business, exclusion happens subtly. The same five people speak in meetings. The same senior leaders shape narratives. Juniors are told to "listen and learn." Feedback flows in one direction, up. Whole identities and backgrounds are left at the door under the guise of "professionalism."

A resilient village refuses this. It treats inclusion as defense. Because when more voices are heard, falsehoods get challenged earlier. Bias gets spotted. Deception gets questioned.

Inclusion isn't charity. It's a strategy. The more diverse the opinions are at the table, the harder it is for a werewolf to dominate the conversation. They may try. But someone will ask, "Wait, that doesn't add up."

Villages that listen widely see more clearly.

Tenet 5: Shared Purpose – Knowing Why the Village Exists

The last and perhaps most unshakable tenet is shared purpose. In Werewolf, games often fall apart when villagers lose sight of what they're trying to achieve. Fear overtakes logic. Ego overtakes empathy. The mission, survival, and truth, forgotten in the scramble for control.

In business, this happens every day. People chase titles instead of impact. Teams compete for budget rather than collaborate for outcomes. Leaders hoard power instead of growing successors.

Shared purpose realigns the village. It reminds everyone why they're here, not to beat each other, but to build something together. Not to win at the expense of others, but to serve something larger.

Purpose must be more than posters and quarterly themes. It must be embedded in hiring, in feedback, in promotions. It must shape how meetings are run, how success is defined, and how leaders are evaluated.

When a village knows its purpose, manipulation becomes harder. People can tell when a leader's agenda doesn't match the mission. And wolves, however smooth, struggle to fake alignment when the villagers are grounded in a deeper truth.

The Village Remembers

Resilient villages don't forget their history. They don't erase the damage wolves have caused. But they use that memory to protect the future.

They teach new employees not just policies, but stories.

They share the lessons of past failures.

They speak the names of those who stood for the right thing and those who didn't.

Memory becomes part of the immune system. It doesn't live in compliance checklists. It lives in culture.

Because what the werewolf fears most is a village that knows itself, that sees clearly, speaks freely, learns openly, includes deeply, and acts with purpose.

That is the only way to win.

Not by catching the wolves.

But by building a village where wolves cannot thrive.

The Other Side of the Moon – A Future Beyond Werewolves

In every game of Werewolf, once the wolves are exposed and removed, the game ends. Victory is declared, and the village breathes a sigh of relief. But in real life, leadership doesn't end with the defeat of toxic actors. Organizations don't just need safety, they need direction, meaning, and renewal. They need a kind of leadership that doesn't simply spot deception, but renders it obsolete.

This is where most companies falter. Once the crisis passes, they celebrate survival and return to business as usual. But if we stop at survival, we remain vulnerable. We rebuild the same patterns. We leave the village walls cracked, waiting for the next werewolf to arrive smarter, smoother, and perhaps wearing a different title.

To truly move forward, we must cross to the other side of the Moon, a place beyond the binary of wolf and villager. A place where leadership isn't defined by charisma, control, or cunning, but by clarity, courage, and connection. A place of Lunar Leadership.

Lunar Leadership: What It Is and Why It Matters

In the mythos of the werewolf, the Moon plays a dual role: it reveals and transforms. Under its light, the hidden is exposed. But it also activates the curse. The very symbol that uncovers truth also provokes darkness. This paradox is at the heart of every organization struggling to evolve.

Lunar Leadership embraces this tension. It's a model of leadership that understands shadow and light, that sees people not as pawns or threats, but as complex beings shaped by fears, hopes, and unseen stories. The Lunar Leader does not rely on manipulation, nor do they pretend that darkness doesn't exist. Instead, they create conditions of light, environments where people can see clearly, think bravely, and act collectively.

Where the werewolf exploits ambiguity, the Lunar Leader creates transparency.

Where the werewolf silences dissent, the Lunar Leader invites challenge.

Where the werewolf performs power, the Lunar Leader distributes it.

This shift isn't aesthetic. It's systemic. It rewires how decisions are made, how success is defined, how power flows, and how truth is treated inside the organization.

From Power Players to Lunar Guides

Let's revisit a familiar character: the corporate alpha, the power player who commands attention, drives results, and inspires both admiration and fear. On the surface, this individual is irreplaceable. But dig deeper and you'll find a trail of burnout, a culture of blame, and a graveyard of good ideas that never survived the weight of ego.

In werewolf terms, this is the dominant player whose voice drowns out the village. Even when they aren't the wolf, they're creating the perfect environment for one. The fear they instill , often unintentionally , suppresses intuition, questioning, and alignment. People conform instead of contributing.

A Lunar Leader, on the other hand, doesn't need to dominate the room. Their strength is not volume or presence, but gravity, a quiet pull that aligns others, not through fear, but through trust. They act more like a guide than a gatekeeper.

They ask better questions. They create pauses instead of filling them. They hold space for contradictions. They're emotionally fluent enough to say, "I don't know," and secure enough to let others shine.

These are the people who turn tense meetings into learning moments, who make juniors feel seen, who catch signs of burnout before metrics reflect it. They notice silences. They adjust tone. They reflect more than they react.

They aren't saviors. They're mirrors. And that subtle shift from control to reflection is how the spell of the werewolf is finally broken.

Full Moon Events: How True Leaders Are Revealed

Ironically, many leaders are revealed not by performance reviews or public keynotes but in moments of crisis, contradiction, or ambiguity. These are what we call Full Moon Events, organizational flashpoints where true character is exposed.

Consider these examples:

- A manager is informed of misconduct involving a high-performing team member. Do they fairly investigate the claim or protect the performer?

- A leader is told their behavior has made someone uncomfortable. Do they dismiss the feedback or sit with it, even if it stings?

- An executive realizes that the goal was set based on flawed assumptions. Do they double down to protect their ego or acknowledge the error and reset?

In each of these moments, the Moon rises, the light is stark, the shadows long. Werewolves panic in this light. They bluff, deny, distract, or manipulate.

Lunar Leaders, though, breathe in that light. They pause. They lean into discomfort. They open space for voices that don't often speak. They use the moment not to preserve themselves, but to reinforce the culture. Their humility is not a tactic, it's a practice.

Organizations must learn to recognize and reward behavior in these Full Moon Events. Too often, we celebrate the charming wolf who wins quarterly results but leaves a wreckage of trust behind. What if, instead, we began to honor the leaders who calm a room without taking control? Who says "I was wrong" without a PR plan? Who speaks up not to dominate, but to protect the village?

This is how the story changes. When Full Moon behavior becomes the standard, not the exception.

How Do You Build for This?

Transformation can't be personality-driven. It must be architectural.

To build Lunar Leadership across an organization, you need to embed its values into four critical systems:

1. Hiring: Stop hiring for polish and prestige. Start hiring for presence, self-awareness, listening skills, and moral courage. Use scenarios that test for ethical ambiguity, not just technical skills.

2. Promotion: Move beyond output metrics. Evaluate how leaders lead. Do their teams feel safe? Do they speak up in retros? Are issues surfaced early or buried?

3. Learning & Development: Train leaders not just in management techniques but in psychological fluency. Teach them how to hold space, spot fear, and cultivate distributed accountability.

4. Feedback Loops: Build robust mechanisms for bottom-up insight. Ensure leaders are regularly hearing feedback from peers, subordinates, and customers. And make it safe to surface uncomfortable truths.

These aren't add-ons. They are cultural infrastructure. Without them, the village will remain vulnerable, no matter how many wolves you unmask.

A Future Village: What It Looks Like

Now imagine a company where fear has no currency.

A place where meetings begin with silence, not because people are scared, but because they're thinking, and they know their thoughts will be heard.

A place where the highest-paid person isn't the loudest, but often the last to speak.

A place where people ask not, "What will this make me look like?" but "What will this do for us?"

This is the future village. It is not utopia. It still has tensions, mistakes, and conflict. But its core is resilient. Its muscles are trained. Its heart beats for truth, not theatrics.

In this village, the werewolf might still show up.

But they'll find the lanterns already lit.

The voices are already strong.

The people are already connected.

And they'll find, much to their dismay, that fear can no longer feed them.

A Final Reflection

The point of the Werewolf analogy is not just to dramatize toxic leadership. It's to remind us that we all play roles, and we all have choices.

At times, we may have been villagers, reacting, confused, silent.

At times, we may have worn the werewolf's mask ourselves, exaggerating, politicking, hiding fear behind aggression.

But we also hold within us the potential to become Lunar Leaders, to move beyond the game. To reshape the story. To redefine what it means to lead.

Because in the end, the strongest village is not the one that wins the game.

It's the one that refuses to play by fear's rules.

And that, finally, is the beginning of leadership.

Chapter 8: Conclusion

It brings the central metaphor of the Werewolf game full circle, offering insight, inspiration, and clear-eyed truth about leadership in a world riddled with manipulation, silence, and unseen influence. It repositions the reader as a changemaker, one who can recognize the dynamics, navigate them wisely, and lead ethically in spite of them.

In the quiet of the boardroom's hum,

Where silence often weighs like stone,

A whisper walks on woven lies,

And fear is dressed in friendly tones.

A nod too quick, a truth delayed,

A smile that hides a sharpened blade,

In daylight deals, in metrics scored,

The werewolves pass the audit board.

But lanterns lit from soul and spark

Can mark the path when all is dark.

For in each heart a village grows,

Guided by a lunar glow.

So take your place, don't wait for the call,

The moon is high. Expose it all.

The game is done. The masks unmade.

It's time to lead, not just evade.

The Game Ends. The Leadership Begins.

The Werewolf game ends when the werewolves are found. But real life doesn't hand out closure. In business, the wolves often don't confess, and the damage they leave behind isn't counted in lives, but in lost innovation, silent meetings, resigned talent, and eroded trust.

This book has used the Werewolf game as a lens, a dramatized mirror for what happens in far too many organizations. Hidden agendas, silenced voices, arbitrary rules, manipulative power structures, and leaders who aren't interested in truth, only loyalty.

The metaphor isn't meant solely to intrigue; it's meant to awaken. Because the game is being played around us every day.

But here's the kicker: you're no longer just a villager.

You're now aware.

You see the patterns, the tells, the traps.

You recognize that true leadership isn't just about exposure.

It's about prevention.

It's about design.

It's about building a culture so resilient, so self-aware, that the wolves simply can't survive there.

This, dear reader, is your invitation, not to win the game, but to change the entire board.

Applying Werewolf Lessons to Real-World Leadership

The Werewolf game teaches us about power, psychology, and trust dynamics. But what do those lessons look like when the chairs are leather, the stakes are financial, and the wolves wear Prada?

Let's unpack the top learnings:

1. Fear Is a Strategy, But It's Not Leadership.

Wolves thrive on fear. They survive by creating confusion, turning suspicion into silence, and forcing quick decisions under pressure. Sound familiar? In the workplace, fear-based leadership still works, but only for short-term gains. Over time, fear calcifies into disengagement, erodes risk-taking, and builds cultures where no one tells the truth.

The solution isn't to become a stronger wolf. It's to dismantle the incentives for deception altogether. This starts with emotional safety, psychological transparency, and leaders who model courage and imperfection.

2. Silence Is Consent, Especially in Leadership.

In the game, villagers lose when they stay quiet. In real life, silence from leadership is perceived as approval. If you're not speaking up about toxic behavior, you are empowering it; if you're not protecting dissent, you're enabling wolves, whether or not you see yourself as one.

True leadership requires uncomfortable clarity. You cannot build trust while protecting politeness over principle.

3. Perception Management Isn't the Same as Truth.

The best wolves in the game aren't aggressive; they're charming. In real life, too, manipulation often wears a likable face. Corporate illusionists use complexity, jargon, and shifting metrics (the "floating goalpost" or "the corporate baton") to distract from outcomes.

As a leader, you need to clarify your definitions of success. Be ruthless with clarity because "clarity is kindness". Reward results that matter, not optics. Measure culture, not just revenue. Track retention, not just recruitment.

4. Systems Reward Patterns, Change the System.

Werewolves win because the game is designed to reward deception. Similarly, corporate systems, when left unchallenged, reward output over integrity, consensus over courage, and performance over process.

If you want a resilient village, you need to build resilient systems:

- Hire for values and courage, not polish

- Promote those who create a positive customer experience, not just results

- Embed feedback loops that surface hard truths early

Change doesn't come from charisma. It comes from intentional infrastructure.

The Balance Between Power and Ethics

Power itself isn't the problem. In fact, leadership requires power. What matters is how it's earned, distributed, and used. In the Werewolf game, wolves hoard power. Villagers try to survive. But in a transformed organization, power becomes a tool for collective flourishing.

- Ethical power is transparent. It can be questioned, audited, and reallocated.

- Ethical power is accountable. It comes with responsibilities, not just privileges.

- Ethical power listens. It doesn't dominate the space; it expands it for others to contribute.

As a leader, ask yourself: Does my power amplify others or silence them? Do people speak more freely in my presence, or less? Do I know the truth of my team, or just the filtered version they think I want?

These questions aren't optional. They're essential to the village's survival.

Thriving in a Corporate World Full of Hidden Agendas

You will encounter Werewolves.

Not just the obvious ones who gaslight and exploit, but the subtle ones. The master illusionists. The middle managers who shift blame expertly. The senior leaders who know the truth but hide behind performance numbers. The consultants who sell culture decks without changing anything.

You can't avoid them.

But you can outgrow them.

Thriving in a world of hidden agendas isn't about playing the game better. It's about building a different village.

Here's how:

- Anchor your leadership in values, not purely metrics. Goals change. Numbers lie. But values are stable ground.

- Protect the truth-tellers. Make heroes of the dissenters, not the loyalists.

- Light the full moon often. Create rituals that reveal what's hidden, retrospectives, anonymous pulses, skip-level meetings, and honest debriefs.

- Invite the hesitant voices. The ones who observe more than they speak often hold the sharpest insights.

- Take off your mask. Admit when you're wrong. Model humility. Because leadership isn't perfection, it's presence and perseverance.

Go Ahead, Build the Resilient Village

There's one final truth from the Werewolf game: the village survives when it works together.

When it values open communication over certainty. When it listens more than it judges. When it pauses before accusing. When it shines the light, not to punish, but to understand.

The resilient village is not a fantasy.

It's your organization, if you choose to design it that way.

And leadership? It's not a crown. It's a lantern.

Go ahead. Pick it up. Light the way. Build the village. Lead the change. Break the spell.

Because the moon is rising. And it's time.

Verses Kindler Publication

Verses Kindler Publication

Reach us through our website -

https://www.verseskindlerpublication.com/

For more information visit our

Instagram or Facebook page.